Student Book 2

Third Edition

Person to Person

Communicative Speaking and Listening Skills

Jack C. Richards   **David Bycina**   **Ingrid Wisniewska**

OXFORD
UNIVERSITY PRESS

OXFORD
UNIVERSITY PRESS

198 Madison Avenue
New York, NY 10016 USA

Great Clarendon Street, Oxford OX2 6DP UK

Oxford University Press is a department of the University of Oxford.
It furthers the University's objective of excellence in research, scholarship,
and education by publishing worldwide in

Oxford New York

Auckland Cape Town Dar es Salaam Hong Kong Karachi
Kuala Lumpur Madrid Melbourne Mexico City Nairobi
New Delhi Shanghai Taipei Toronto

With offices in

Argentina Austria Brazil Chile Czech Republic France Greece
Guatemala Hungary Italy Japan Poland Portugal Singapore
South Korea Switzerland Thailand Turkey Ukraine Vietnam

OXFORD and OXFORD ENGLISH are registered trademarks of
Oxford University Press

© Oxford University Press 2005

Database right Oxford University Press (maker)

Library of Congress Cataloging-in-Publication Data

Richards, Jack C.
  Person to person : communicative speaking and listening skills / Jack
C. Richards, David Bycina, Ingrid Wisniewska.—3rd ed.
    p. cm.
  Contents: Student book 1—Student book 2.
  Rev. ed. of: New person to person student book. New York : Oxford University
Press, c1995-
  ISBN-10: 0-19-430216-4 (student book 2)
  ISBN-13: 978-0-19-430216-6 (student book 2)
  ISBN-10: 0-19-430215-6 (student book 2 with CD)
  ISBN-13: 978-0-19-430215-9 (student book 2 with CD)
  [etc.]
  1. English language—Textbooks for foreign speakers. 2. English language—
Spoken English—Problems, exercises, etc. 3. Oral communication—Problems,
exercises, etc. 4. Listening—Problems, exercises, etc. I. Bycina, David. II.
Wisniewska, Ingrid. III. Richards, Jack C. New person to person student book.
IV. Title.

PE1128.R46 2005
428.3'4-dc22

2004065481

Executive Publisher: Nancy Leonhardt
Senior Acquisitions Editor: Chris Balderston
Senior Editor: Patricia O'Neill
Associate Editor: Amy E. Hawley
Assistant Editors: Hannah Ryu, Kate Schubert
Art Director: Maj-Britt Hagsted
Senior Designer: Claudia Carlson
Art Editor: Elizabeth Blomster
Production Manager: Shanta Persaud
Production Controller: Eve Wong

ISBN-13: 978 0 19 430215 9
ISBN-10: 0 19 430215 6

Printed in Hong Kong.

10 9 8 7 6 5 4 3

ACKNOWLEDGMENTS

Consider This sections written by Lewis Lansford

Illustrations by: Gary Antonetti pp.15 (map), 75, 77, 112; Barbara Bastian pp.25,
51, 61, 69, 103, 108, 110, 111, 114; Kathy Baxendale pp.13, 47, 53, 55, 56, 89,
105 (sports); Martha Gavin pp.4, 26 (theater), 82, 95; Neil Gower pp.11, 12, 17,
63, 73, 76, 107; Mike Hortens pp.15 (directory), 24, 27 (posters), 50, 64, 68, 105
(posters); Jon Keegan pp.9, 30, 37, 38, 42, 43, 83, 87, 93, 102, 106, 113; Eric
Larsen pp.16, 67; Colin Mier pp.52, 91; Karen Minot pp.31, 46, 65, 99; Sandy
Nichols pp.34, 39, 79; Geo Parkin pp.3, 29, 35, 41, 81, 94, 109

Cover photograph by: Dennis Kitchen Studio

Location and studio photography by: Dennis Kitchen Studio pp. 2, 6, 10, 14, 18, 22,
28, 32, 36, 40, 44, 48, 54, 58, 62, 66, 70, 74, 80, 84, 96, 100; Kjeld Duits pp. 88,
92

The publishers would like to thank the following for their permission to reproduce photo-
graphs: Alamy: BananaStock p.18 (talking on cell phone); Brand X Pictures p.5
(students working); Cheapshots p.57 (ladle); Chris McLennan p.88 (skysurfer);
David Cook/blueshiftstudios.co.uk p.90 (hang gliding); Design Pics Inc. p.7 (tennis); Dynamic Graphics Group p.2 (shaking hands); IML Image GroupLtd pp.69,
111 (fancy hotel); Lanny Ziering p.7 (rock band); Leslie Garland Picture Library
p.57 (kettle); Maxiilian Weinzierl p.57 (cake pan); Paul Springett p.90 (bungee
jumping); Photofusion Picture Library p.19 (teen on cell); SCPhotos p.71
(Victoria Peak); Swerve p.57 (waffle iron); Wilmar Photography.com p.90 (kite
surfing); Bettmann/CORBIS p.96 (Bruce Lee); Jonathan Blair/Corbis p.7 (making
pizza); Claudia Carlson pp.36 (elderly reunion), 18 (text message); Foodpix p.57
(blender); Laca Trovato p.57 (rice cooker); Jules' Undersea Lodge p.62 (undersea
lodge); Photodisc Green pp.22 (receptionist), 57 (coffee machine, chopping
board), 72 (Fiji); Photodisc Green/Jack Hollingsworth p.28 (woman on cell);
Robert Harding World Imagery p.71 (Old Chinatown); Stone pp.70 (Sydney
Opera House), 72 (Kenya safari); Jess Koppel p.44 (lemon slice); Taxi/Anne
Ackerman p.7 (chess); Chris Ladd p.72 (Rome); Tim Hall p.80 (restaurant); The
Image Bank/Grant Faint p.10 (Grand Bazaar)

Special thanks to: City University of New York Graduate Center, The New York
Public Library Science, Industry and Business Library

The publishers would like to thank the following people for their help in developing this new
edition: Laura MacGregor, Tokyo, Japan; Su-Wei Wang, Taiwan; and Max
Wollerton, Tokyo, Japan.

The publishers would like to thank the following OUP staff for their support and assistance:
Satoko Shimoyama and Ted Yoshioka.

Welcome to *Person to Person*. Let's take a look at the sections of the units.

Conversations — The two conversations present examples of the language you will be studying. You can listen to them on the CD in class or at home.

Give It a Try — This section teaches the language points from the conversations. You will focus on each one separately and then practice them with a partner.

Listen to This — The listening section gives you real-life listening tasks that help you review your understanding of the language from the unit. You answer questions or complete charts about the listening.

Let's Talk — These are pair- or group-work activities that ask you to expand on what you have learned. You can use both the language you have learned and your imagination.

Consider This — "Consider This" presents some interesting facts on a cultural topic related to the theme of the unit. You can use these facts as an introduction to the unit.

Pronunciation Focus — A pronunciation point related to the language from the unit comes after Conversation 2. This helps you to practice the language in the unit in a more natural way.

Person to Person — These pages present a problem based on the language from the unit. You and a partner will work together to solve the problem, using the language you have learned, as well as your own ideas and opinions.

In addition to the language presented in each unit, here are some expressions that will be very useful to you—both inside and outside of class.

1. Please say that again.
2. I'm sorry. I don't understand.
3. Please speak more slowly.
4. How do you say _____ in English?
5. What does _____ mean?
6. I don't know.
7. May I ask a question?
8. How do you spell _____?

We hope you find that learning to speak and understand English is easier than you think. Good luck!

Contents

Conversation 1
Haven't we met before?

Where can you make friends with people who speak English? Make a list of places.

Bow. Shake hands. Kiss. Hug.

People around the world greet one another in different ways.

In...	People often greet each other with...
Canada	a handshake
Thailand	a nod with palms together
France	two or three kisses on both cheeks
China	a nod or slight bow

- How do you usually greet your friends?
- What about people you meet for the first time?

Class CD 1, Track 2

Pete:	This is a great film festival, isn't it?
Liz:	It sure is. This film looks wonderful.
Pete:	Yes, it does. Have you been to this film festival before?
Liz:	Yes, I was here last year.
Pete:	This is my first time. You know, you look familiar. Haven't we met before?
Liz:	I'm not sure.
Pete:	I think we were in the same computer class last year. With Ms. Clark?
Liz:	I remember you now!
Pete:	My name's Pete. Pete Wilson.
Liz:	I'm Liz Wu. It's good to see you again. Sorry I didn't recognize you at first.
Pete:	Well, my hair was a lot longer then, and I wore glasses.

Student CD, Track 2

GIVE IT A TRY

1. Conversational openings

This is a great film festival, isn't it?	It sure is. This film looks	wonderful.
	Yes, it is. This film looks	very interesting, doesn't it?
It sure does.		
Yes, it does.		

PRACTICE 1

Class CD 1
Track 3

Listen to the example. Then start a conversation by choosing one of the openings below. Reverse roles.

Openings
1. It's a great party.
2. The food here looks delicious.
3. It's an exciting concert.
4. This course sounds interesting.

Responses
1. The music is good.
2. The desserts are fantastic.
3. I love this music.
4. The teacher is really good.

PRACTICE 2

Take turns starting a conversation in the situations below. Think of as many conversational openings for each situation as you can.

Use These Words

crowded	busy
slow	late
exciting	delicious
fantastic	nice

2. Extending the conversation

| Have you been to this film festival before? | Yes, I was here last year. |
| | No, this is my first time. |

| Is this the first time you've been to this film festival? | Yes, it is. I'm enjoying it a lot. |
| | No, I was here last year. |

PRACTICE

Class CD 1
Track 4

Listen to the example. Then take turns starting a conversation in the situations below. Make each conversation as long as possible.

1. at a tennis match
2. at a rock festival
3. in a soccer stadium
4. at a yoga class
5. at a judo competition
6. on a flight

3. Asking if you've met before

Haven't we met before? I think we've met before, haven't we? Don't I know you from somewhere?	I'm not sure. | Have we? | Do you?
I think we met at Sam's birthday party. Weren't you at Sam's birthday party? You were at Sam's birthday party, weren't you?	Oh, yes. I remember you now. Yes, that's right. No, I don't think so. I think you have the wrong person.
My name's Pete. Pete Wilson.	I'm Liz Wu.

PRACTICE 1

Class CD 1 Track 5

Listen to the example. Then ask your partner if you've met before. Use the information below and introduce yourselves.

1. met at Kathy Chan's party
2. used to be neighbors
3. belong to the same gym
4. take the same train in the mornings
5. sat next to each other at a rock concert
6. your idea _____

PRACTICE 2

Walk around the class and start conversations with other students. Talk about where you met before (your facts can be true or false).

LISTEN TO THIS

Class CD 1 Track 6

Part 1 Listen to three conversations. Where are they? Write the correct number of the conversation next to each place.

___ at a friend's wedding   ___ at a high school reunion   ___ in a class

Part 2 Listen again and write the names of the people and the details of where they met.

	Names	Where did they meet?
1		
2		
3		

Part 3 Listen to the conversational openings again. Think of some alternative openings for each situation.

Part 1 On a piece of paper, write three sentences about places or events you have been to.

- I went to Saitama High School.
- I stayed at the Raffles Hotel in Singapore last year.
- I studied in England for one year.

Part 2 Work in pairs. Give your piece of paper to your partner. Use the information from the piece of paper to ask if you have met before. Continue the conversation until your teacher says *Stop talking*. Switch partners.

Part 3 What interesting facts did you learn about your classmates? How much can you remember about each person? Tell the class.

Conversation 2

I've heard a lot about you.

What topics do you usually talk about when you first meet someone? Make a list.

Class CD 1, Track 7

Luis:	Hey. Sorry I'm late.
Liz:	That's OK. We just got here. Luis, this is my friend Eun-joo. Eun-joo, this is Luis. We met in class last year.
Eun-joo:	Hi, Luis. Nice to meet you.
Luis:	Hi, Eun-joo. I've heard a lot about you.
Liz:	Luis just got back from Hong Kong.
Eun-joo:	Really? How was it?
Luis:	It was amazing.
Liz:	You went to a rock concert there, didn't you?
Luis:	Yeah, my friends are in a band, so they gave me free tickets.
Eun-joo:	I hear you're a good bass player.
Luis:	I'm not bad. But I haven't played that much recently. Do you play music?
Eun-joo:	Yes, I do. Actually, my friends are having a jam session this weekend. Do you want to come?
Luis:	Sounds cool!

Student CD, Track 3

Class CD 1, Track 8
Pronunciation Focus

Listen to the rise and fall of the intonation in these sentences.

Luis, this is my friend Eun-joo.
Eun-joo, this is Luis.

Listen to the conversation again and notice the intonation.

GIVE IT A TRY

1. Introducing friends

A:	Luis, this is my friend Eun-joo. Eun-joo, this is Luis. We met in class last year.		
B:	Hi, Luis.	(It's) nice (I'm) glad (It's) good	to meet you.
C:	Hello, Eun-joo.	(It's) nice (I'm) glad (It's) good	to meet you, too.

PRACTICE

Class CD 1 Track 9

Listen to the example. Work in groups. Then introduce one friend to another. Use first names. Take turns making the introductions.

2. Making small talk (1)

I hear you're a good bass player.	I'm not bad. Do you play music?
Yes, I do. I play keyboards. No, I don't. / I'm afraid I don't.	How often do you play?
Whenever I can. / Every weekend.	

PRACTICE

Class CD 1 Track 10

Listen to the example. Then ask your partner about the following activities. Reverse roles.

① musician / play music

② chess player / play chess

③ cook / like cooking

④ tennis player / play sports

3. Making small talk (2)

A: Luis just got back from Hong Kong.	
B: Really? How was it?	C: It was amazing.
B: How long were you there?	C: Just five days.
B: What did you do there?	C: I went to a rock concert.

PRACTICE

On a separate piece of paper, quickly write down:
1. something you did recently
2. the last place you visited
3. the last movie you saw
4. the last concert you went to

Class CD 1 Track 11 Listen to the example. Work in groups. Student A uses one of the items Student B wrote to introduce him or her to Student C. Student C continues the conversation by asking questions.

> **Use These Words**
>
> | | |
> |---|---|
> | fantastic | depressing |
> | awesome | awful |
> | wonderful | scary |
> | cool | weird |
> | beautiful | crazy |

LISTEN TO THIS

Class CD 1 Track 12 *Part 1* Listen to three conversations. Write the main topic of each conversation in the chart.

Part 2 Listen again and write the first names of the people and how you think they are related to each other.

	Main topic	Names	Relationship
1			
2			
3			

Part 3 Which conversations were more formal? Which were informal? Which were friendly? Were any unfriendly? How do you know?

(Students A and B look at this page. Students C and D look at page 106.)

Part 1 Students A and B read the information below. Imagine that you and your partner meet at a party for new students. Make small talk and find out three interesting facts about your partner.

Student A: Samuel / Samantha Wong
Your information:
You went to high school in the U.S.
You like all kinds of sports, especially swimming.
You recently visited relatives in Australia.
You think that you met Student B at a film festival last weekend, but you don't remember his or her name.

Student B: Christopher / Christine Suzuki
Your information:
You were on the soccer team in high school.
You love music, especially techno and rap.
You recently went rock climbing in India.
You think that you met Student A at a film festival last weekend, but you don't remember his or her name.

Now Try This

Make new groups of four. Introduce your partner to the other two students. Add some information about your partner. It can be true or false. Your partner agrees or disagrees. Continue the conversation.

Part 2 Now work with Students C and D. Everyone takes turns introducing his or her partner to the rest of the group. The rest of the group asks questions to continue the conversation.

Conversation 1
Where can I get this cleaned?

Describe what is happening in the picture. How do you think these people are feeling?

CONSIDER THIS

The world's first shopping mall

The Grand Bazaar in Istanbul, Turkey, is the world's oldest shopping mall.
—Built in the 1400s
—More than 4,000 shops and restaurants
—More than 331,000 square meters of shopping

What can you buy there?
antiques, books, carpets, rugs, ceramics, jewelry, leather goods, maps, prints, silk, wood products... and thousands of other things!

● Where would you like to go shopping?

Class CD 1, Track 13

Sandy: Watch out! Oh no, you got coffee on your shirt.
Mari: Just my luck! What am I going to do now? I've got my violin recital this afternoon.
Sandy: I could lend you a spare T-shirt if you want.
Mari: Thanks, but I really need this shirt. Do you know where I can get it cleaned? It has to be really fast.
Sandy: Well, I think there's a dry cleaner's in the mall across the street. Or you can try the dry cleaner's on Washington Street. It's next to the King Building.
Mari: OK, I'll try the mall first. Where was the other one?
Sandy: It's a small dry cleaner's next to the King Building on Washington. About two blocks from here.
Mari: Which one is the King Building?
Sandy: It's that big glass office building just past the park. It has a green glass dome on the top.
Mari: OK. Maybe I'll just go buy a new shirt in the mall, what do you think?
Sandy: That might be faster!

Student CD, Track 4

1. Asking where services are located

| Excuse me. | Where can I get my shirt cleaned? |
| | Do you know where I can buy a new shirt? |

(I think) there's a dry cleaner's	in the mall across the street.
	on the corner of Lincoln Avenue and Lee.
You can try the store on Washington Street. It's	next to the King Building.
	about two blocks from here.

PRACTICE 1

Class CD 1 Track 14

Listen to the example. Then ask your partner where you can run three of the following errands. Your partner will look at the map to find the answers. Reverse roles.

1. check your e-mail
2. get your watch fixed
3. get your coat cleaned
4. mail a package
5. buy some aspirin
6. get a spare key cut

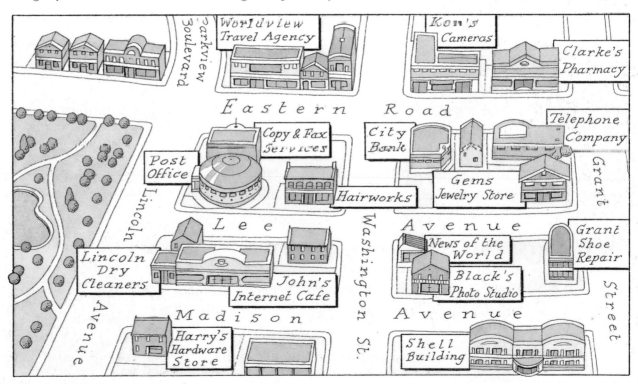

PRACTICE 2

Class CD 1 Track 15

Listen to the example. This time ask your partner where you can run three of these errands. Your partner will look at the map to find the answers. Reverse roles.

1. send a fax
2. get your picture taken
3. buy an airline ticket
4. get your hair cut
5. get some cash
6. get your shoes repaired

2. Describing buildings

> Which one is the King Building?
>
> It's the big glass office building just past the park.

PRACTICE

Class CD 1
Track 16

Listen to the example. Student A covers the information for Student B. Student A asks Student B about three of the following buildings. Student B will describe the building and say where it is located. Reverse roles.

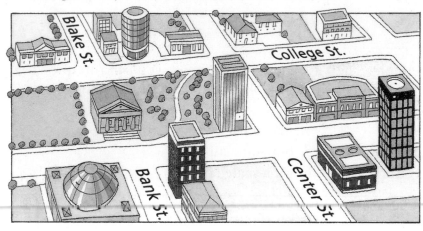

Use These Words

across from	next to
near	just after
just before	on the corner
between	behind

Student A
1. the Police Station
2. the Science Museum
3. the Grant Bank Tower
4. the Italian Embassy
5. the Center Department Store
6. the City Reference Library

Student B
1. short red brick building
2. old gray stone building with pillars
3. round glass tower
4. short orange building
5. tall red brick building
6. tall black office tower

LISTEN TO THIS

Class CD 1
Track 17

Part 1 Listen to the conversation between Kumiko and her friend Bruce. What does Kumiko want to buy?

Part 2 Listen again and write the letter of the building next to the correct name.
___ Metro Hotel   ___ Manning Building
___ Sports World   ___ Manulife Building

Part 3 Describe the location of each building in the picture. What do you think is in each building?

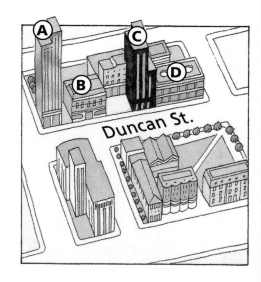

Part 1 Choose one of the services below and write it in the chart.

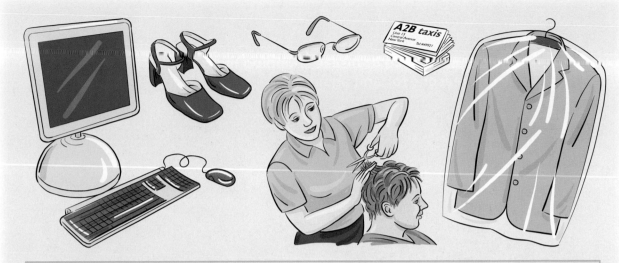

Name of service: _____

Person's name	Name of place	Location	Building description

Part 2 Walk around the class and ask ten people where they would get the service done.

Part 3 Present the results of your survey to the class. Which place was the most popular?

Conversation 2
Where can I find a clothing store?

Why do people like or dislike shopping malls? Make
a list of reasons for and against.

Class CD 1, Track 18

Clerk:	Could I help you?
Mari:	Yes, could you tell me where I can find a women's clothing store?
Clerk:	There are several women's clothing stores in the mall. There's one on this level, about four stores down from here on your right, just past the drugstore.
Mari:	Thanks a lot!
Clerk:	Yes?
Woman:	Is there a hairdresser in this mall?
Clerk:	Yes, there's one on the third floor. Take the escalator up two flights.
Woman:	Thank you.
Man:	I'm looking for an umbrella. Where can I find them, please?
Clerk:	The best place is Field's Department Store, on the second floor.

Student CD, Track 5

Class CD 1, Track 19
Pronunciation Focus

Listen to the consonant
groups in these words.

clothing   dru**gst**ore
u**mbr**ella   e**sc**alator

Listen to the conversations
again and notice the
consonant groups.

1. Asking for directions in a store (1)

> Could you tell me where I can find an umbrella?
>
> In the accessories department, on the second floor.

PRACTICE

Class CD 1
Track 20

Listen to the example. Then take turns asking your partner where you can do each of the following things in the store. Use information from the store directory.

1. buy a bracelet
2. get some perfume
3. exchange a man's sweater
4. look at video games
5. buy a tablecloth
6. have lunch

Field's Store Directory

Accessories	2	Jewelry	1
Children's wear	2	Men's fashions	2
Customer service	5	Perfume	1
Electronics	5	Restaurant	5
Furniture	5	Rest rooms	3,5
Health and beauty	1	Toys	4
Home furnishings	4	Women's fashions	3

2. Asking for directions in a store (2)

> I'm looking for an umbrella. Where can I find them, please?
>
> Umbrellas are on this floor. Walk down here to your left. They're across from the perfume counter.

PRACTICE

Class CD 1
Track 21

Listen to the example. Think of things you can buy in a department store. Take turns asking your partner where you can buy the things. Use the information from the floor plan.

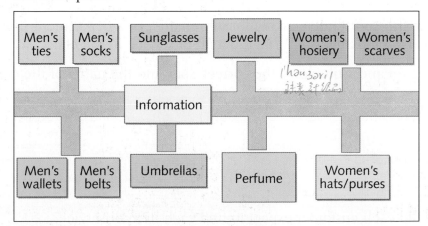

Use These Words

socks	belt
gloves	wallet
sunglasses	scarf
hat	watch
tie	purse

3. Asking for directions in a mall

I need to buy a new shirt.	Where can I find Can you tell me where I can find	a women's clothing store?
There is a women's clothing store	on this level. on the third level. about four stores down, just past the drugstore.	

PRACTICE

Class CD 1
Track 22

Listen to the example. Then take turns asking and answering questions about places in the mall.

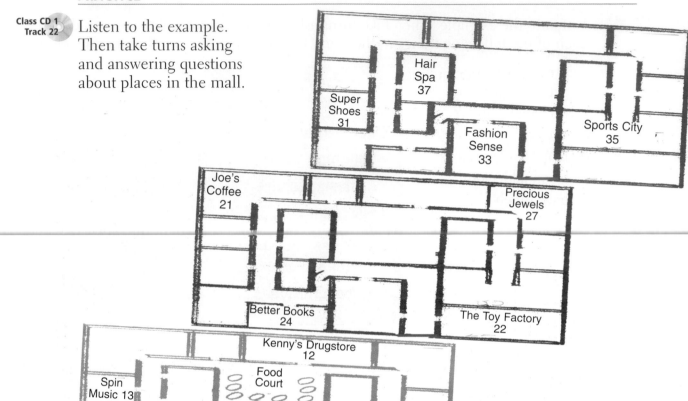

LISTEN TO THIS

Class CD 1
Track 23

Part 1 Listen to three customers asking for information in a department store. What is each person looking for? Write the item or service in the chart.

Part 2 Listen again and write down the correct floor and the name of the department.

	Item or service	Floor	Department
1			
2			
3			

Part 3 Where did each customer expect to find each item or service?

(Student A looks at this page. Student B looks at page 107.)

Part 1 You have recently moved to the town on the map below. Ask questions to find out where you can do the following. Write the names of the places on the map.

1. buy books
2. get your car fixed
3. make photocopies
4. get your clothes dry-cleaned
5. buy ice cream
6. get your prescription filled

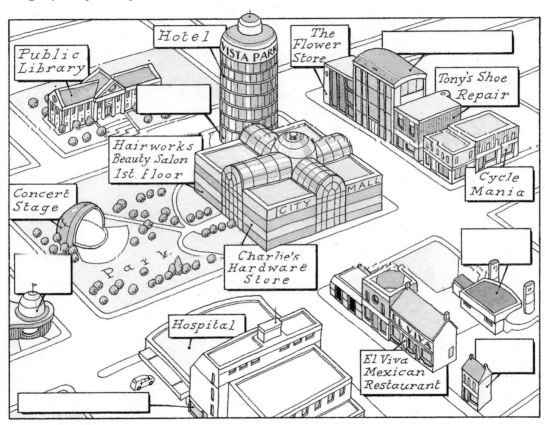

Part 2 Student B has also recently moved to the town. Answer his or her questions about where to find some goods and services.

Now Try This

Choose two or three places in your neighborhood that provide goods and services. Tell your partner where they are and how to recognize where they are located.

Conversation 1
Could I please speak to Jo?

Do you prefer phone calls, e-mails, or text messages? What are the advantages of each one?

Class CD 1, Track 24

Jo:	Hello.
Hong-an:	Could I please speak to Jo?
Jo:	Speaking.
Hong-an:	Hi, Jo. This is Hong-an. Listen, I'm having a party at my place this Friday night. Are you free?
Jo:	Sure! What time?
Hong-an:	Anytime after 8:00.
Jo:	Great! See you Friday, then.
Mrs. King:	Hello?
Hong-an:	Hi, Mrs. King. Is John there, please?
Mrs. King:	I'm sorry, he's not here right now. Could I take a message?
Hong-an:	Yes, please. I'm calling to tell him there's a party at my place on Friday, and…
Mrs. King:	Just a moment. Let me get a pen…. All right, go ahead.
Hong-an:	OK. This is Hong-an Li, and my number is 312-364-0107. Could you ask John to call me?
Mrs. King:	Sure. I'll give him the message as soon as he gets in.

Student CD, Track 6

1. Asking to speak to someone

Hello.
Hi.
Could I please speak to Jo?
Is Jo there, please?
Speaking.
Hi, Jo. This is Hong-an.

Hello.		
Hi.		
Could I please speak to Jo?		
Is Jo there, please?		
Sure, just a	moment, please.	
	minute.	
Hold on. I'll get her.		

PRACTICE 1

Class CD 1 Track 25

Listen to the example. Call your partner. Reverse roles.

PRACTICE 2

Class CD 1 Track 26

Listen to the example. Call someone else in the class. Your partner will answer. Reverse roles.

2. Offering to take a message

Hi, could I please speak to John?	I'm sorry, he's not here right now. Could	I take a message?
	Can	
No, thanks. I'll call back later.		
Yes, please.		

PRACTICE

Class CD 1 Track 27

Listen to the example. Student A calls someone in the class. Student B gives a reason why the person can't come to the phone. Reverse roles.

Use These Words

is out of town
isn't home yet
won't be back until 6:00
has gone to see a movie

3. Taking a message

Can I take a message?	Yes, please.
Just a moment. Let me get a pen.... All right, go ahead.	This is Hong-an Li, and my number is 312-364-0107. Could you ask John to call me? Could you tell John I'm having a party on Friday night?
Sure.	I'll give him the message as soon as he gets in. I'll tell him you're having a party on Friday night.

PRACTICE 1

Class CD 1
Track 28

Listen to the example. You are calling John, but your partner answers. Leave a message for him by choosing one of the options below. Reverse roles.

Please tell John…

1. to call me about tonight's homework.
2. I'm having a party on Friday.
3. I can't pick him up tomorrow morning.
4. I need to talk to him about our plans for this Saturday.

PRACTICE 2

Call your partner and leave a message for someone. Use your own ideas. Your partner will repeat the message back to you. Reverse roles.

LISTEN TO THIS

Class CD 1
Track 29

Part 1 Listen to two phone conversations. Write who the messages are for and who the messages are from.

Part 2 Listen again and write the messages.

Part 3 How do you think the people in each conversation are related? How do you know?

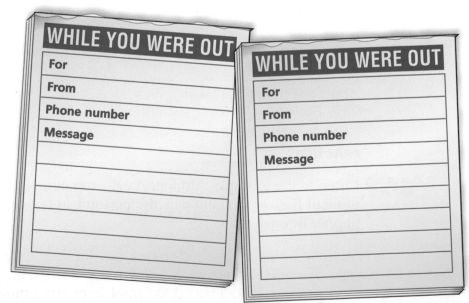

WHILE YOU WERE OUT
For
From
Phone number
Message

WHILE YOU WERE OUT
For
From
Phone number
Message

LET'S TALK

Part 1 Work in groups. Write your name on a piece of paper. Fold it and hand it to one person in another group.

Part 2 You are going to call the person on the piece of paper. Think of a message you want to give to this person and write it down. For example:

My computer crashed and I need your help.

Can you give me a lift home tomorrow?

Can I borrow your bike this weekend?

What is the assignment for tomorrow?

Do you want to go to the movies with me tomorrow night?

I need some help with my homework.

Write your message here:

Part 3 Work in pairs. Place your chairs back to back with someone from your group. Call your partner and leave a message for the student you wrote the message to in Part 2. Your partner will write down the message on a piece of paper. Then reverse roles.

Part 4 When everyone in the class has finished, give the message you took to the correct person. Then find the person you wanted to give a message to. Is the message correct? Talk about the most interesting message.

Conversation 2
I'm sorry. Her line is busy right now.

When you leave a phone message, what information should you always include?

Class CD 1, Track 30

Voice:	*You have reached the English Language Institute. For Admissions, press or say 1 now. If you know…*
Woman:	Good morning. Admissions Office. Can I help you?
Hong-an:	Yes, please. I am interested in taking a language class. Could you tell me how to apply?
Woman:	Yes, of course. You just need to fill out an application form and send it to us with the registration fee.
Hong-an:	Great. Could you send me a form, please? My name is Hong-an Li, H-o-n-g (dash) a-n, L-i, and my address is 4211 South Main Street, Chicago, 60614.
Woman:	OK, we'll send that out to you right away.
Hong-an:	I'd also like some information about student housing.
Woman:	Sure, you can speak to our student housing coordinator. Hold on a moment, please. I'll see if she is available… . I'm sorry, her line is busy right now. Could I have your number?
Hong-an:	Yes, of course. My number is 312-364-0107.
Woman:	I'll see she gets back to you very soon.

Student CD, Track 7

Class CD 1, Track 31
Pronunciation Focus

Listen to the stressed syllables in these words.

1st syllable	**2nd syllable**	**3rd syllable**
institute	ad**mis**sions	appli**ca**tion
interested	a**vail**able	regi**stra**tion

Listen to the conversation again and notice the stressed syllables.

1. Calling for information

I am interested in taking a language class. Could you tell me how to apply?	You just need to fill out an application form and send it to us with the registration fee.
Great. Could you send me a form, please?	OK, we'll send that out to you right away.

PRACTICE

Class CD 1 Track 32

Listen to the example. Then call your partner and ask for information about one of the following. Reverse roles.

1. CAL Airlines / apply for a job as a flight attendant / application form and resume
2. Yoga for Everyone / take a yoga class / application form and registration fee
3. Talent International / enter a music competition / application form, photograph, and sample music CD
4. Global Card Services / apply for a credit card / application form and copy of ID card

> **Use These Words**
>
> Right away.
> No problem.
> Sure.
> That's fine.
> Thanks for your help.
> Don't mention it.
> You're welcome.
> Thank you for calling.

2. Asking for additional information

I'd also like some information about student housing, please.
Sure, you can speak to our student housing coordinator. Hold on, please. I'll see if she is available.

PRACTICE

Class CD 1 Track 33

Listen to the example. Use the situations from the Practice above and role-play the conversations again. This time request additional information from below. Reverse roles.

1. job requirements / human resources manager
2. equipment / yoga instructor
3. competition dates / competition coordinator
4. interest rates / financial advisor

3. Leaving a message

I'm sorry, the housing coordinator's line is busy. Could I have your number?	Yes, of course. My number is 312-364-0107.
I'll see she gets back to you very soon.	

Class CD 1
Track 34

Listen to the example. Student A answers the phone and says the person is not available. Student B asks to leave a message. Include your name, phone number, and the reason for your call. Reverse roles.

Phone Message

For: _Ms. Jones_

From: _Hong-an Li_

Phone: _312-364-0107_

Message: _He would like some information about student housing._

Message taken by: _Brenda_

Student A

1. course manager
2. human resources manager
3. yoga instructor
4. competition coordinator

Student B

1. Josephine Yu / 933-491-0037 / course dates
2. Harold Cutter / 721-603-6721 / job requirements
3. Akiko Matsutani / 492-690-1674 / equipment
4. Sarah Curran / 803-299-5668 / competition dates

PRACTICE 2

Think of three more situations where you might have to leave a formal or recorded message and role-play them with your partner.

LISTEN TO THIS

Class CD 1
Track 35

Part 1 Listen to four phone conversations. What places are they calling? Who does the caller want to speak to? Write the information in the chart.

Part 2 Listen again and write down if the person is available, or not.

	Place called	Who does the caller want?	Available?
1			
2			
3			
4			

Part 3 What was the result of each phone call? Make notes of any useful phrases.

(Student A looks at this page. Student B looks at page 108.)

Part 1 You are the receptionist at Soundz Eazy music recording studio. You answer the phone for Ed Black, an executive at the company. He is not able to come to the phone. Answer the phone and take a message for him.

Soundz Eazy RECORDING STUDIO

FOR _____

DATE _____ TIME _____

WHILE YOU WERE OUT

NAME _____

of _____

PHONE _____

| TELEPHONED | | RETURNED YOUR CALL | | WILL CALL AGAIN | |
| CAME TO SEE YOU | | PLEASE CALL | | WANTS TO SEE YOU | |

MESSAGE _____

_____

_____

_____

_____

Part 2 Mr. Black asks you to call Pete Saito and explain that it is not possible to arrange a meeting today, but he can phone and arrange an appointment for an audition. Your number is 591-555-7899.

Part 3 Answer the call from Pete Saito. Here is some information for new musicians about getting an audition:
1. send a sample music CD and a photograph
2. send a completed application form
3. send in the audition fee
4. for information on renting the studio and sound equipment, call the studio manager

Now Try This

You are a new student calling for information about your school or college. Your partner is the receptionist. Role-play the conversation.

Review:
Units 1–3

LISTEN TO THIS UNIT 1

Class CD 1 Track 36

Listen to the conversation and answer the questions.

1. Where are they? _____
2. Where did they meet before? _____
3. What are their names? _____
4. Did they recognize each other? _____

GIVE IT A TRY

Work in pairs. Choose two famous people. They can be actors, musicians, or sports stars. Imagine that the two people see each other at a party. They have met before. Write a conversation between them about how they met and what they have done recently. Role-play the conversation for the class. The class tries to guess who the people are.

LISTEN TO THIS UNIT 2

Class CD 1 Track 37

Listen to a clerk giving directions at the information desk in a mall. Where is each person going?

1. _____ 2. _____ 3. _____

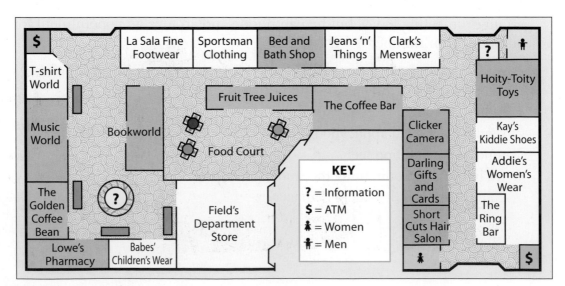

GIVE IT A TRY

Work in groups. Write the name of four stores in your town. What service does each store provide? Where is each store? Write the information in the chart.

Name of store	Service	Location

LISTEN TO THIS UNIT 3

Class CD 1
Track 38

Listen to messages on an answering machine. Fill in the missing information below.

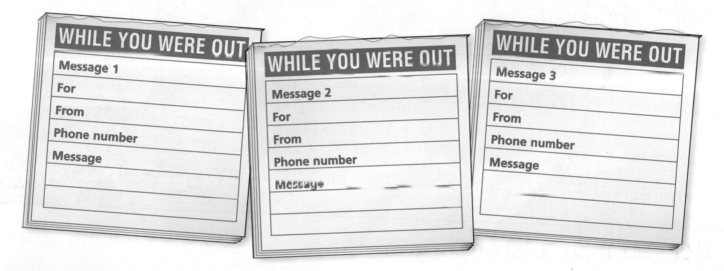

WHILE YOU WERE OUT

Message 1	
For	
From	
Phone number	
Message	

WHILE YOU WERE OUT

Message 2	
For	
From	
Phone number	
Message	

WHILE YOU WERE OUT

Message 3	
For	
From	
Phone number	
Message	

GIVE IT A TRY

Work in pairs. Look at the flyers below. Think of three questions you could ask when you call each place. Then have a telephone conversation with your partner.

Yoga classes
Experienced Teacher
Flexible hours
$15
Tel. 654-555-4202

Sound Bite Live!
Rock Garden
8 P.M. til late
Tickets: 491-555-7865

Improve your English!
Native speaker offers private lessons
Tel: 792-555-9798

Unit 4

Conversation 1
What can we do?

Do you have a cell phone? Make a list of the advantages and disadvantages of having one.

A survey asked *What invention do you hate but can't live without?* The number one answer: the cell phone. People love cell phones because they are convenient, but they hate them because they never allow people to be in peace.

Inventions people love—and hate:
Cell phone—30%
Alarm clock—25%
Television—23%
Shaving razors—14%

- What invention do you hate but can't live without?

Class CD 1, Track 39

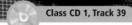

Jane: Is that your cell phone? It's really loud!

Pat: Yeah—sorry, just a minute, I'll turn it off.

Jane: You know, it's really a problem when people bring their cell phones to class. Some students even answer their phones and have conversations while class is going on!

Jim: I know what you mean. It's not polite and it disturbs everyone. What can we do?

Jane: We can have a sign up on the wall, like they do in the movie theater, that says, "Remember to turn off your cell phones."

Pat: That's a good idea, but maybe we could put the sign on the door so you see it before you come into class.

Jim: Let's have a fine for anyone whose phone rings in class.

Pat: Oh, yeah? Like how much? And who would collect the money? That's too complicated.

Jim: We can have a box, and when your phone rings, you put in a quarter. How does that sound?

Pat: Yeah, we can use it to buy drinks for the end-of-semester party!

Jane: Leave it to you to think of that.

Student CD, Track 8

GIVE IT A TRY

1. Identifying a problem

It's really a problem when people bring their cell phones to class.	I know what you mean. It's not polite and it disturbs everyone.

PRACTICE 1

Class CD 1
Track 40

Listen to the example. Then look at the pictures below. Think about why using cell phones in these situations might be a problem. Talk about those problems with your partner. Reverse roles.

Use These Words	
dangerous	risky
harmful	annoying
considerate	loud
noisy	disruptive

PRACTICE 2

Can you think of any other situations where using cell phones might be a problem? Talk about them with your partner. Reverse roles.

PRACTICE 3

Think of some problems in your classroom or school. Discuss them with your partner and say why they are a problem. Choose some of these ideas, and add more ideas of your own.

1. not enough classrooms
2. not enough computers
3. too many students in each class

4. the cafeteria is too expensive
5. the textbooks are expensive
6. your idea _____

2. Making suggestions

A: What can we do? What can we do about students using cell phones in class?	B: We can have a sign on the wall that says, "Remember to turn off your cell phones."
A: That's a good idea. That would work.	C: Let's have a fine for anyone whose cell phone rings in class.
A: That's too complicated. That wouldn't work.	

Class CD 1
Track 41

Work in groups. Listen to the example. Look at the pictures from Practice 1 in Part 1. One student in the group will ask about solutions to the problems. The other two students will each make one suggestion. The first student will decide if the suggestions are good, or not, and why.

PRACTICE 2

Work in groups. Which of these issues are problems in your neighborhood or town? Discuss the problems and make suggestions.

too many cars / not enough buses

streets are badly lit / crime is increasing

too crowded / too expensive

too much garbage or trash / not enough parks

LISTEN TO THIS

Class CD 1
Track 42

Part 1 An environmentalist is discussing ways of protecting the environment. Listen and write down the four main problems she mentions.

Part 2 Listen again and make notes of her solution for each problem.

	Problems	Solutions
1		
2		
3		
4		

Part 3 What does "Think Green" mean? Compare your answers with a partner.

Part 1 Work in groups. Think of a problem in your school that affects everyone. In the chart, write three reasons why it is a problem.

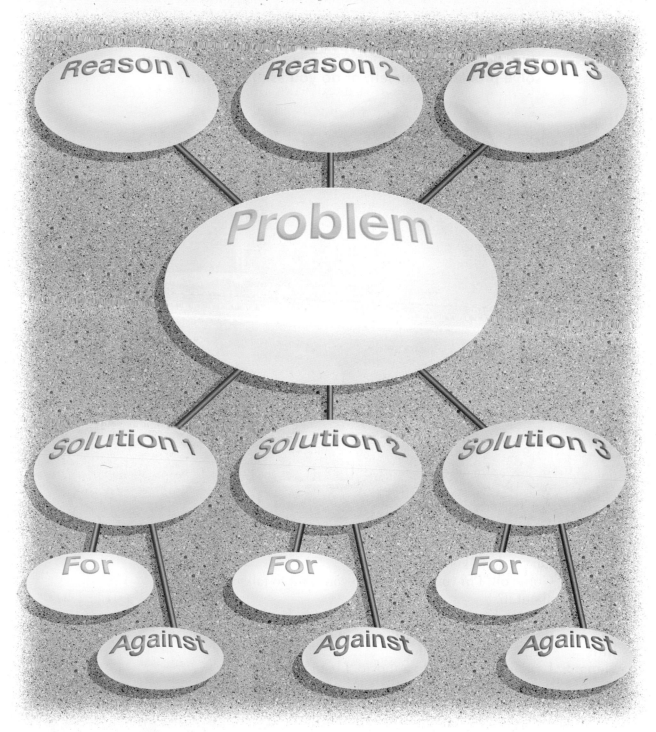

Part 2 In your group, think of three different solutions and why they would or would not work. Then take a vote on the best solution.

Part 3 Tell the class about the results of your discussion. Find out if the rest of the class agrees or disagrees.

Conversation 2
What would you do?

Who do you talk to when you have a problem? Do you solve problems yourself, or do you ask for advice?

Class CD 1, Track 43

Jim:	OK, Tamara, what's the problem?
Tamara:	Oh…I don't know.
Jim:	Come on, I'm your friend—do you want to talk about it?
Tamara:	OK. It's Ken. He's really fun to be with, but he's the cheapest guy I've ever gone out with.
Jim:	Why? What did he do?
Tamara:	Last night we went to a movie. I bought the tickets while he parked the car.
Jim:	So?
Tamara:	Well, he never gave me any money for his ticket. Then he went to the snack bar and came back with popcorn and soda…for himself! He never even asked me if I wanted anything!
Jim:	Wow! That sounds pretty bad.
Tamara:	I know. I really like him, but he makes me so mad. What should I do?
Jim:	You should start looking for a new boyfriend!

Student CD, Track 9

Class CD 1, Track 44
Pronunciation Focus

The intonation in *Wh-* questions usually falls. In Yes/No questions, it usually rises. Listen to these questions.

What's the problem?

Do you want to talk about it?

Listen to the conversation again and notice the intonation of the questions.

1. Asking for and giving advice

What's the	problem?	Ken is the cheapest guy I've ever gone out with.
	matter?	What should I do?
What are you upset about?		I don't know what to do.

Why don't you talk to him about it?	
You should	start looking for a new boyfriend!
If I were you, I'd...	

PRACTICE 1

Class CD 1
Track 45

Listen to the example. Student B has a problem. He or she explains the problem to Student A and asks for advice. Student A chooses the best advice from the suggestions below or uses his or her own idea.

Student B's problems

1. your math grades are not good
2. you share a room with your brother or sister and he or she snores
3. you're gaining weight; your clothes don't fit
4. you saw your boyfriend/girlfriend holding hands with someone else

Student A's suggestions

- wake him or her up
- ask him or her about it
- start exercising
- buy some earplugs
- go on a diet
- study more
- break up with him or her
- your idea _____

PRACTICE 2

Reverse roles and repeat Practice 1.

Student A's problems

1. your brother or sister takes your things without asking
2. your best friend owes you money
3. you are always tired in class
4. your parents are too strict

Student B's suggestions

- tell your parents how you feel
- go to bed earlier
- ask the friend to lend you money
- ask him or her to pay you back
- tell your parents
- drink coffee before class
- ask your parents to change their rules
- your idea _____

2. Describing consequences

Ken is the cheapest guy I've ever gone out with. What should I do?	Why don't you talk to him about it?
If I criticize him, he'll get mad at me!	In that case, I think you should start looking for a new boyfriend!

PRACTICE 1

Class CD 1
Track 46

Listen to the example. Then choose one of the problems from the previous practices. Respond to your partner's advice by describing the consequence of his or her advice. Your partner will give additional advice. Reverse roles.

PRACTICE 2

Work in groups. Each of you will describe an everyday problem and get advice from the other members of your group. Respond to each suggestion by describing the consequences.

I have a problem and I don't know what to do...

Use These Words

Good idea!
I suppose I should.
I haven't tried that.
That wouldn't work.
That's no good.
I've tried that and it didn't work.

LISTEN TO THIS

Class CD 1
Track 47

Part 1 Listen to three conversations between people asking their friends for advice. Write the problems in the chart.

Part 2 Listen again and write the advice.

	Problem	Advice
1		
2		
3		

Part 3 What questions does each person ask to find out if there's a problem? Make a list.

(Student A looks at this page. Student B looks at page 109.)

Part 1 Your partner is a counselor. You are going to talk to him or her about the problem below. Read the description of the problem carefully and then explain it. Answer any questions your counselor asks. Listen carefully and write down his or her suggestions.

Your problem:

You want to take a year off when you finish school to travel through Europe with your friend. You want to visit all the famous art museums in Paris, Rome, and London. You could practice your English! You'd learn a lot about art. You want to be an artist one day. Your parents are really against you going to Europe, though. They say it's dangerous. They say you should settle down and find a job and start earning some money so you can save up to buy a house.

Suggestions:

1. _____

2. _____

3. _____

Part 2 You are now a counselor for your partner. Listen carefully to his or her problem. Ask questions so that you understand the problem completely. Then give three suggestions about what your partner should do.

Part 3 Do you like the suggestions that your partner gave? Discuss with your partner why each one would or would not work.

Now Try This

Think of a real problem that you had in the past. How did you solve it? Tell your partner about the problem and see what advice he or she can suggest. Then compare the advice with what really happened.

Conversation 1
Haven't you heard yet?

How often do you speak with friends? How do you stay in touch?

 Class CD 1, Track 48

Young-hee: Have you heard about Eun-mi?

Jung-soo: No, I haven't talked to her in a while. How are things with her?

Young-hee: Well, so-so. She broke her arm.

Jung-soo: That's terrible. How did it happen?

Young-hee: Well, she went skiing during winter vacation. She had a bad fall and broke her arm.

Jung-soo: That doesn't sound so good, but I'm glad it wasn't worse. How's she doing with her schoolwork?

Young-hee: Haven't you heard yet? She's decided to drop out of college and become a musician.

Jung-soo: You're kidding! What made her decide to do that?

Young-hee: Well, you know that CD she made in her home recording studio? She sent it to a record company and they're giving her a contract!

Jung-soo: That's great news! Good for her. Maybe she'll be on TV soon!

1. Asking about other people

Have you heard about Eun-mi?	No, I haven't.	How's she doing these days? How are things with her?

Not too good. So-so. / Not bad. Pretty good. / Great.		

Have you heard about Eun-mi?	No, I haven't.	What's happening with her? What's she doing these days?

She broke her arm. She's going to become a pop star.		

PRACTICE

Class CD 1 Track 49

Listen to the example. Take turns asking and answering questions about the people below.

Emily	Marco	Chen	Akiko

2. Reacting to good and bad news

She broke her arm.	That's terrible. I'm sorry to hear that. I'm glad it wasn't worse.

She's going to become a pop star.	That's great news! Good for her. I hope it works out well.

PRACTICE

Class CD 1 Track 50

Listen to the example. Take turns asking and answering questions about the people from the Practice above.

3. Asking for more details

| She broke her arm. | How did it happen? |
| She decided to drop out of college. | Why did she decide to do that? |

PRACTICE 1

Class CD 1 Track 51

Listen to the example. Ask your partner about each of the people below. Be sure to ask for more details. Reverse roles.

Use These Words

luckily	fortunately
unfortunately	the other day
recently	in the end
at the time	finally

① Wanda

② Sam

③ Tim

④ Yumi

PRACTICE 2

Think of a famous person and talk about him or her with your partner. Tell your partner some recent news about that person. Reverse roles.

LISTEN TO THIS

Class CD 1 Track 52

Part 1 Listen to three different conversations. What is the main topic of each conversation?

Part 2 Listen again and decide if it was good or bad news.

	Topic	Good news or bad news?
1		
2		
3		

Part 3 What words and phrases in each conversation tell you that it was good or bad news?

Part 1 Work in pairs. Tell your partner a piece of good news and a piece of bad news that has happened to you recently. Then react to your partner's news. Ask each other questions to find out more details.

Part 2 Work in pairs. Ask a new partner about the news from his or her first partner. React to the news and ask for as many details as you can. Then reverse roles.

Part 3 Tell the class about the good news and bad news you found out. Is all your information correct?

Conversation 2
Wait a minute. Was she hurt?

Do you have friends who like to talk about other people? Why do some people like to gossip?

Class CD 1, Track 53

Young-hee:	Did you hear about *The People Next Door*?
Yumi:	No, what happened?
Young-hee:	Well, let me tell you! Brenda caught Stan—that's her boyfriend—kissing another woman.
Yumi:	That's terrible! She should have left him right away!
Young-hee:	She did! She ran out, got in the car, and drove away.
Yumi:	The poor woman! So, where did she go?
Young-hee:	She ended up at the hospital. She was…
Yumi:	Wait a minute. Why did she go to the hospital?
Young-hee:	She was driving too fast and had an accident. Anyway…
Yumi:	She shouldn't have driven so fast. Was she hurt?
Young-hee:	She broke her arm. But listen, the important thing is that she fell in love with the doctor who fixed her arm. Now, as soon as she feels a little better, they're going to start dating.
Yumi:	Let me get this straight. Brenda caught Stan with another woman, got into a car accident, and now she's going out with her doctor?
Young-hee:	That's right.
Yumi:	That's unbelievable. It sounds like a soap opera.
Young-hee:	Yumi. It *is* a soap opera. It's called *The People Next Door*. It's on TV every day at noon.

Student CD, Track 11

Class CD 1, Track 54
Pronunciation Focus

Listen to the stressed and unstressed words in these sentences.

Where did she go?
Was she hurt?

Listen to the conversation again and notice the stressed and unstressed words.

1. Saying what someone should have done

Did you hear about Brenda?	No, what happened?
Brenda caught Stan kissing another woman.	She should have left him right away! She shouldn't have stayed with him.

PRACTICE

Class CD 1 Track 55 Listen to the example. Take turns asking about each person below and saying what they should or shouldn't have done.

Michael   Jane   Jin   Atsuko

2. Asking for details

She was driving too fast and had an accident.	Was she hurt?

She fell in love with the doctor who fixed her arm.	Did she tell him about her boyfriend?

PRACTICE

Class CD 1 Track 56 Listen to the example. Tell your partner about the people below. Your partner will ask for more details. Answer the questions using your own ideas. Reverse roles.

Student A
1. Trudy and Angela / won the lottery
2. Hideo / dropped out of college
3. Ken / was on TV last night
4. Ben and Sachiko / going to Nepal
5. Tran and Jackie / went to Australia
6. your idea _____

Student B
1. Did they win a lot of money?
2. Did he get a job?
3. Was he on a game show?
4. Are they going to Mount Everest?
5. your idea _____
6. your idea _____

3. Interrupting and getting back to the story

Did you hear about Brenda? She ended up at the hospital. She was…	Wait a minute. Why did she go to the hospital?
She was driving too fast and had an accident. Anyway…	Was she hurt?
She broke her arm. But listen, the important thing is that she fell in love with the doctor who fixed her arm.	Let me get this straight. Brenda caught Stan with another woman, got into a car accident, and now she's going out with her doctor? That's unbelievable.

PRACTICE

Class CD 1
Track 57

Listen to the example. Then choose one of the stories below and tell it to your partner. He or she will interrupt you and ask questions. Answer and return to telling the story. Finally, your partner will repeat the story to you. Reverse roles.

> **Use These Words**
>
> That's…
> incredible   unbelievable
> weird   amazing
> crazy   strange
> wonderful   fantastic

1. your friend Mimi / moved to Germany / joined a rock band / fell in love with the lead singer / got married

2. your uncle Jim / gave up his job / won $1 million in a lottery / got married / lives in Mexico

3. your friend Scott / sold his house / got a job in San Francisco / the company went bankrupt / he's moving back to New York

4. your idea _____

LISTEN TO THIS

Class CD 1
Track 58

Part 1 Listen to a story about two mountain climbers. Number the pictures in the correct order.

Part 2 Listen again. What questions did the woman ask about the story?

Part 3 What do you think Dave and Meg should have done?

Part 1 Work in pairs. Put the following pictures in the correct order.

Emergency rescue.

Part 2 Using the pictures, take turns telling each other the story.

Part 3 With your partner, discuss what you think the people in the story should have done. Then tell the class your suggestions. Which suggestions were the most interesting?

Now Try This

Think of an amazing story that happened to you or a friend. Write the story in six sentences. Write each sentence on a different piece of paper. Give the sentences to a partner. He or she will put the story together. Then ask what the people in the story should have done.

Conversation 1
I feel terrible.

What do you think is wrong with this man? Describe his symptoms.

 Class CD 1, Track 59

Li-wei:	You look a little feverish. Are you OK?
Jay:	To tell you the truth, I feel terrible.
Li-wei:	Why? What's the matter?
Jay:	I have a horrible headache and a sore throat.
Li-wei:	Did you take anything for it?
Jay:	I took some aspirin, but it didn't do any good. I feel awful. My whole body aches.
Li-wei:	Why didn't you call the doctor?
Jay:	I thought I might feel better after a good night's sleep, but I feel worse this morning.
Li-wei:	You know, there's a pretty bad flu going around. Maybe you shouldn't go to class today.
Jay:	But I have a test this afternoon!
Li-wei:	Why don't you call the doctor and see what she says? You'd better take your temperature first. Then maybe you should lie down.
Jay:	That's a good idea. I think I'll lie down for a while.

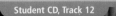 Student CD, Track 12

1. Talking about symptoms

You look a little feverish. Are you OK?	To tell you the truth,	I feel terrible. I don't feel very well.
Why? What's the matter?	I have a horrible headache and a sore throat.	

PRACTICE

Class CD 1
Track 60

Listen to the example. Then choose four of the situations below. Talk about your symptoms with your partner. Reverse roles.

1. pale / splitting headache
2. sick / awful stomachache
3. tired / couldn't sleep last night
4. flushed / horrible cough
5. ill / bad toothache
6. terrible backache / can't move

2. Giving, accepting, and refusing advice

You should take some aspirin. Why don't you take some aspirin? You'd better take some aspirin.	Maybe you're right. That's a good idea. I'll give it a try. I took some aspirin, but it didn't do any good. I tried that, but it didn't help.

PRACTICE

Class CD 1
Track 61

Listen to the example. Then choose four of the situations below. Talk about your symptoms with your partner. Your partner will give some advice. Reverse roles.

1. sore throat
2. backache
3. cut on hand
4. fever
5. cough
6. your idea _____

Use These Words

cough drops	heating pad
cough syrup	ice pack
aspirin	bandage

3. Advising someone *not* to do something

| You look terrible. What's the matter? | I have a horrible headache and a sore throat. |
| Maybe you shouldn't go to class today. | But I have a test this afternoon! |

PRACTICE

Class CD 1
Track 62

Listen to the example. Then use the cues below to talk about your symptoms with your partner. Your partner will give you advice. Continue the conversation with your own ideas. Reverse roles.

Student A
1. can't sleep
2. a sunburn on my face
3. a sore throat
4. red eyes
5. shoulder pain
6. a stomachache
7. a twisted ankle
8. your idea _____

Student B
1. don't drink coffee
2. don't go out in the sun
3. don't talk too much
4. don't use the computer
5. don't lift anything
6. don't eat anything
7. your idea _____
8. your idea _____

LISTEN TO THIS

Class CD 1
Track 63

Part 1 Listen to a conversation between Tracy and Jake. What is wrong with Jake?

Part 2 Check (✓) which of these remedies are mentioned in the conversation.

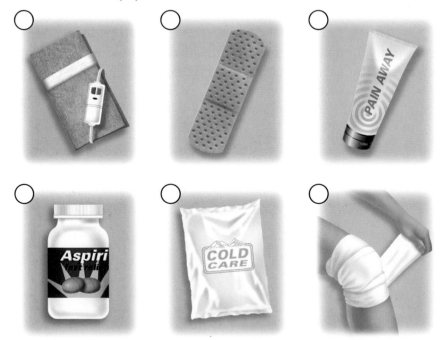

Part 3 Which remedies does Jake finally agree to try?

Part 1 Choose one of the problems below and write it in the chart.

- heartburn
- nosebleed
- headache
- cold
- hiccups
- sunburn

- dizziness
- stomachache
- toothache
- jet lag
- earache
- sore throat

Part 2 Imagine that you have that problem. Walk around the class and ask your classmates for a remedy. Write the remedies in the chart.

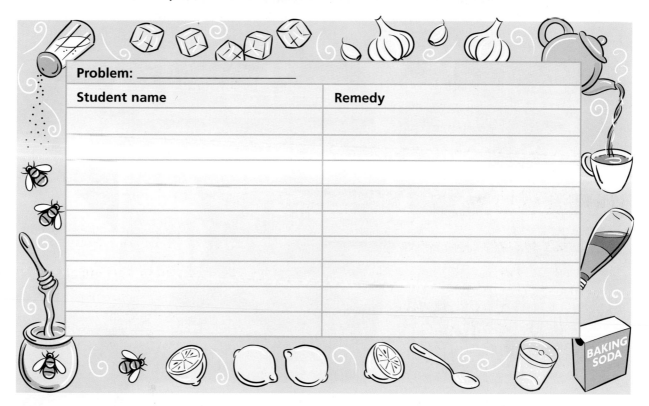

Problem: _____	
Student name	**Remedy**

Part 3 Tell the class about the remedies you wrote in the chart. Which ones were the most popular?

Conversation 2
What do you think I should take?

What do you take when you have a cold or the flu?

Class CD 1, Track 64

Pharmacist: Can I help you?

Jay: Hmm…Yes, please. I think I have the flu and I have a big test this afternoon. What do you think I should take? Can you recommend something, please?

Pharmacist: What are your symptoms?

Jay: I have a terrible headache, a sore throat, and a fever.

Pharmacist: That sounds like the flu. You could try a non-prescription pain reliever and fever reducer. Take two tablets every six hours, with food. That should help. If your fever doesn't come down within 24 hours, you should see your doctor.

Jay: Are there any special instructions?

Pharmacist: Yes, you must take these with food. And you can't drink any alcohol. Are you allergic to aspirin?

Jay: No, I'm not.

Pharmacist: You'll be fine then.

Jay: OK, I'll take those and a package of cough drops, please.

Pharmacist: That'll be $15.50.

Class CD 1, Track 65
Pronunciation Focus

Listen to these phrases. Which words are not stressed?

allergic to aspirin
a package of cough drops

Listen to the conversation again and notice the pronunciation of the prepositions.

Student CD, Track 13

1. Asking for advice

What do you think I should take for a headache? What do you recommend for a sore throat?	You could try I recommend	this pain reliever. these cough drops.

PRACTICE

Class CD 1
Track 66

Listen to the example. Then take turns talking about the problems below.

1. played tennis yesterday / leg and arm muscles are stiff today
2. it's cold and flu season / worried about getting sick
3. on the computer a lot recently / my eyes are dry and red
4. went jogging this morning / have a twisted ankle
5. ate spicy food for lunch / have terrible heartburn
6. have bad allergies / allergy pills make me drowsy
7. your idea _____
8. your idea _____

Use These Words

eye drops	muscle relaxer
vitamins	ankle brace
antacid	allergy pills

2. Giving instructions

How often do I have to take it?	Take two tablets every six hours, with food. Your fever should come down within 24 hours. / If the fever doesn't come down within 24 hours, you should see your doctor.

PRACTICE

Class CD 1
Track 67

Listen to the example. Then take turns talking about the problems from the previous Practice. Student A will ask for advice. Student B will be the pharmacist. The pharmacist will give instructions for how to use the medicine. Reverse roles.

3. Asking about instructions

Are there any special instructions?	You must take these with food. You can't drink alcohol.

Am I allowed to take aspirin with this medication?	No, you shouldn't take any aspirin.

Look at the drug warning labels below and decide with your partner what they mean. Then match the labels with the list below.

1. Take all the medicine.
2. Do not touch your eyes with this.
3. Shake the bottle first.
4. Chew this medicine.

5. Take this with a meal.
6. Don't eat or drink this.
7. Keep this away from children.
8. Don't sit out in the sun.

PRACTICE 2

Class CD 1 Track 68 Listen to the example. Then take turns asking and answering questions about the medicines in Practice 1.

PRACTICE 3

Talk with your partner about three medicines. Discuss what you must do and must not do when taking those medicines.

LISTEN TO THIS

Class CD 1 Track 69 *Part 1* Listen to a pharmacist talking to three customers. Listen and write down the problem in each case.

Part 2 Listen again and write down what each customer buys.

	Customer's problem	What did they buy?
1		
2		
3		

Part 3 What instructions does the pharmacist give each customer?

(Student A looks at this page. Student B looks at page 110.)

Part 1 Student B suffers from insomnia (inability to sleep). Think of a few possible solutions to this problem and make a list. Then listen carefully to your partner's problem. Recommend the best remedies from your list. Answer any questions about special instructions for using these remedies.

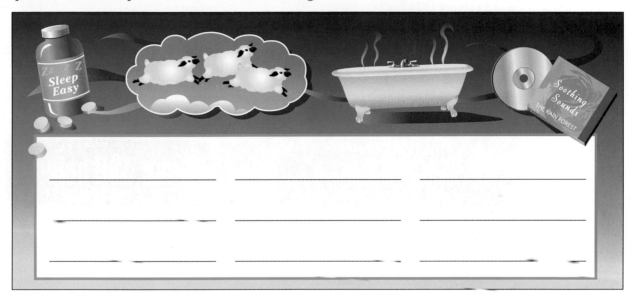

Part 2 You suffer from frequent migraines (strong and painful headaches). For the past week, you have had migraines every day for at least two or three hours. You have tried all kinds of painkillers and they don't work. You don't like to take very strong painkillers because they make you sleepy. Tell Student B your problem. Listen to your partner's suggestions, choose the best one, and ask about any special instructions.

Write the suggestion here:

_____

Part 3 Work in groups. Compare the suggestions each person chose in your group. How many people had the same suggestion?

Now Try This

Think of a common health problem that you or someone you know has had. Tell your partner about the problem and ask for advice.

Review:
Units 4–6

LISTEN TO THIS UNIT 4

**Class CD 1
Track 70**

Someone is discussing the problem of too many cars in cities. Listen and write down the three effects of this problem and the three solutions that are mentioned.

Effects	Solutions

GIVE IT A TRY

Work in groups. Choose one of the problems below. Explain your problem to the rest of the group. Each person in the group will give you some advice. Who gave you the best advice? Give that person one point. Continue the game, using your own ideas.

1. I feel nervous before tests.
2. I always oversleep.
3. I have too much homework.
4. My parents don't like my boyfriend / girlfriend.
5. I spend too much money.
6. your idea _____

LISTEN TO THIS UNIT 5

**Class CD 1
Track 71**

Listen to three conversations. Fill in the chart.

	Who?	Main topic	Good news or bad news?
1			
2			
3			

Work in groups. Choose one of the newspaper headlines below. Use your own ideas to make notes about the details of the story. Tell your story to your group. The people in your group will respond to the story, ask for details, and say what the person in the story should have done.

$500 Stolen from Bicycle Outside Bank

Car Hit by Train at Traffic Crossing

Helicopter Rescue from Arctic Ice Storm

Poisonous Snake Escapes from City Apartment

LISTEN TO THIS UNIT 6

Class CD 1 Track 72

Listen to Shami talking about her symptoms. Write them in the chart below. Which remedies has she tried and which ones has she not tried? Write the answers in the chart.

Shami's symptoms	Remedies Shami has tried	Remedies Shami hasn't tried

GIVE IT A TRY

Work in pairs. Write questions you can ask about how to use each item below. Then ask your partner the questions.

What do you do with old furniture and clothes you don't need? Make a list.

Class CD 2, Track 2

Denise: Thanks for helping me clean out the garage.

Terumi: I'm glad to do it. It's interesting.

Denise: Wow! The people in my family are real collectors! They never throw anything out.

Terumi: You're not kidding. What's this thing?

Denise: It's an old ice-cream maker, I think.

Terumi: How do you use it?

Denise: Let's see if I can remember...oh, yeah. First, you put this metal container in the bottom of the tub. Then you fill it with an ice-cream mixture made from eggs, sugar, and milk. Next, you put the lid on the metal container and fill the rest of the tub with ice and salt.

Terumi: What's next?

Denise: After that, you turn this handle, and you keep adding salt and ice until you can't turn the handle any more.

Terumi: And then what?

Denise: You open it up, and there's your delicious homemade ice cream.

Student CD, Track 14

1. Describing what objects are used for

| What's this thing? | It's an ice-cream maker. |

| What's this thing used for? | It's used | for making ice cream. |
| | | to make ice cream. |

Class CD 2
Track 3

Listen to the example. Student A chooses one object and asks what it is used for. Student B answers by using the cues below.

Student A

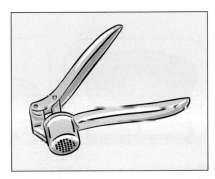

garlic press

steamer basket

wok

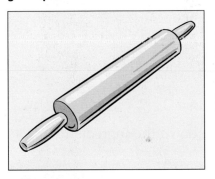

rolling pin

pasta maker

rice cooker

Student B
- steam-cook food
- cook rice
- crush garlic

- make fresh pasta
- fry meat and vegetables
- roll out pastry

Work in groups. Think of an object that is used in your kitchen. Describe what it is used for. The others in your group will guess the name of the object. Each person takes a turn.

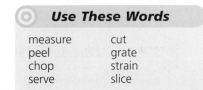

Use These Words	
measure	cut
peel	grate
chop	strain
serve	slice

2. Giving instructions

How do you	use	it?	First, you put this metal container in the bottom of the tub.
	make		Then you fill it with an ice-cream mixture.
Please show	me how to	use	it.	Next, you put the lid on the container and fill the rest of
tell		make		the tub with ice and salt.
How does it work?			After that, you turn this handle.

PRACTICE 1

Listen to the example. Work in pairs. Take turns explaining how to use the objects in the pictures from Practice 1 in Part 1.

PRACTICE 2

Put the steps of how to make an omelette in the correct order. Then take turns telling your partner how to make it.

____ add mixture to frying pan and cook for five minutes

____ melt butter in a frying pan

____ add salt and pepper and bit of milk

____ beat three eggs in a bowl

LISTEN TO THIS

Part 1 You will hear a recipe. Listen and write down the ingredients.

Part 2 Listen again and write the instructions.

Ingredients	Instructions
	Step 1
	Step 2
	Step 3
	Step 4
	Step 5
	Step 6
	Step 7

Part 3 What tools do you need for this recipe?

Part 1 Work in groups. Choose one of the items below. Without speaking, show how to use it. The rest of the group should try to guess what the item is for.

For example:

A: (acts like he or she is pouring water into a kettle)

B: It's for boiling water.

A: Correct! It's a kettle.

kettle

rice cooker

chopping board

ladle

blender

coffeemaker

waffle iron

cake pan

Part 2 Work in pairs. Choose an item from above. Take turns explaining how to use it. Then reverse roles.

Part 3 Work in pairs. Choose an item not on this page. Without speaking, show how to use it. Your partner will try to guess what it is. Reverse roles.

Conversation 2
What else do I need?

Do you ever have picnics? What things do you or your family usually take?

Class CD 2, Track 6

Denise: Hey, Terumi, would you like to go to the beach for a barbie with us next weekend?

Terumi: A barbie, what's that?

Denise: It's a barbecue! We'll cook food for everyone at the beach. Look, our outdoor grill is right here.

Terumi: I'd love to come. Do I need to bring anything?

Denise: Well, you'll need a hat and some sunscreen. You could get badly sunburned out there. You might also need some insect repellent.

Terumi: What do I need insect repellent for?

Denise: It's to keep mosquitoes and other insects away. They're attracted by the smell of the food.

Terumi: OK. What else do I need?

Denise: That's it, really. But we'll also be taking an esky.

Terumi: What's an esky?

Denise: It's for keeping drinks cool!

Terumi: Oh, a cooler!

Denise: Yeah! And some charcoal, here it is…oh yes, and a fire extinguisher! Just in case!

Student CD, Track 15

Class CD 2, Track 7
Pronunciation Focus

Words ending in a [t] sound are often linked to words beginning with a consonant. Listen and practice these phrases.

next weekend
get sunburned
insect repellent
That's it, really.

Listen to the conversation again and notice the linked words.

1. Discussing needs and requirements

Do I need to bring anything?	Yes, you need a hat. No, not really.
What else do I need?	You might also need some insect repellent. That's it.

PRACTICE

Class CD 2 Track 8

Listen to the example. Invite your partner to do one of the activities below. Your partner will ask what he or she needs to bring. Suggest two or three things. Reverse roles. Write down the things your partner suggests.

1. surfing _____
2. picnic _____
3. weekend camping trip _____
4. skiing trip _____
5. one-day hiking trip _____
6. your idea _____

Use These Words

knife	sunglasses
map	candles
flashlight	sleeping bag
raincoat	water bottle

2. Asking for clarification

What do I need insect repellent for?	It's to keep mosquitoes and other insects away.

What is the esky for?	It's for keeping drinks cool.

Why do we need a fire extinguisher?	Just in case!

PRACTICE 1

Class CD 2 Track 9

Listen to the example. Then look at the items your partner suggested in the previous Practice. Ask your partner why you need each one. Reverse roles.

PRACTICE 2

Student A is going to have a birthday party next Saturday night. Student B asks Student A what he or she needs to bring to the party and why. Reverse roles.

3. Talking about consequences

| Why do I need a hat? | If you don't wear a hat, you'll get sunburned. |

| Why do I need insect repellent? | You should use insect repellent, otherwise / or you'll get bitten by mosquitoes. |

PRACTICE 1

Class CD 2
Track 10 Listen to the example. Student A lives in Australia. Student B is going to visit Student A for two weeks in August. Suggest four or five things he or she should bring and explain why they are needed.

PRACTICE 2

Student B lives in Alaska. Student A is going to visit Student B for two weeks in August. Suggest four or five things he or she should bring and explain why they are needed.

LISTEN TO THIS

Class CD 2
Track 11 *Part 1* Heidi is going to visit her friend Nicki in Aspen, Colorado, for a week. Listen to them discussing what Heidi needs to bring. Write down the activities they are planning.

Part 2 Listen again and write the items Heidi needs to bring.

Activities	Items

Part 3 Why does Heidi need to bring each item?

Part 1 Your partner is a visitor from another country and wants to find out about your culture. Choose one of the topics below. You are going to explain how to make or prepare it. First, make a list of all the tools that you need. Then make a list of the steps (at least four).

- how to prepare a typical dish
- how to make a decoration for a festival or holiday
- how to make a traditional craft

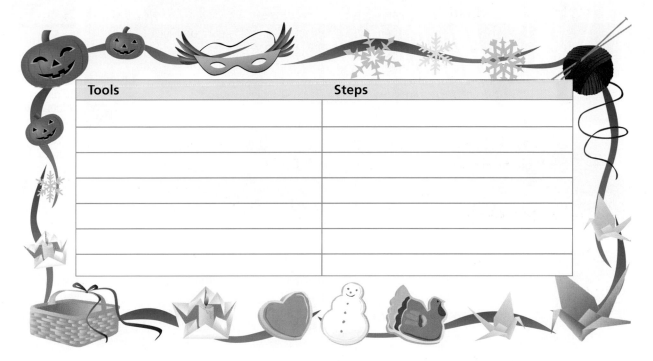

Tools	Steps

Part 2 Now tell your partner how to make or prepare the thing you chose. First, explain each tool and what it is used for. Then give the instructions. Answer any questions. Make sure he or she understands the process clearly.

Part 3 Reverse roles. Your partner will explain how to make or prepare a typical food, decoration, or craft. You will take notes about each step and ask questions. Draw a picture if it is helpful.

Now Try This

Use your notes to show your classmates each step of making or preparing the food or craft without saying anything. First, they will try to name each instruction as you act it out. Then they will guess what you are making.

Conversation 1
We'd like to book a hotel.

What kind of hotels do you like to stay in when you travel? Make a list of the most important features.

Jules' Undersea Lodge

This small hotel in Florida has hot showers and television—but only two bedrooms and no doors. How do you get in? By diving seven meters underwater and swimming up through a hole in the floor!

● Would you like to stay in Jules' Undersea Lodge?

Class CD 2, Track 12

Agent: Can I help you?

Julie: We'd like to book a hotel in Tioman for one week.

Agent: Are you interested in a hotel or a package?

Lisa: Well, we'd like to learn how to scuba dive so the package would be better, I think.

Agent: I see. Do you want to stay in a budget hotel or a luxury resort?

Julie: Mm, something in the middle, I think.

Agent: OK. Take a look at this brochure.

Julie: Where is this hotel?

Agent: Oh, it's right on the beach.

Lisa: This looks perfect. We'd like to reserve a double room from September 23–30.

Agent: Certainly. I just need your names, please.

Student CD, Track 16

1. Asking about types of hotels

We'd like to book a hotel in Tioman, please. Can you recommend a hotel in Tioman, please?	Are you interested in	a hotel a resort	or a package?
Well, a | package | would be better. | hotel	Take a look at this brochure		
This looks | perfect. | a bit too expensive.			

PRACTICE

Class CD 2
Track 13

Listen to the example. Student A is planning a one-week trip to Tioman. Ask Student B for advice. Student B is a travel agent. Help Student A choose a hotel. Reverse roles.

Spa Resort HOTEL RATING ★ ★ ★

SET ON A SECLUDED BEACH, ideal for swimming, diving, and snorkeling.

SINGLE AND DOUBLE STORY BUNGALOWS surrounded by palm trees and gardens, most within a 2-minute walk of the beach.

SHARED BATH and shower facilities.

OPTIONAL DIVING packages and boat excursions.

White Sands HOTEL WS RATING ★ ★ ★ ★

Single story apartments with one, two, or three bedrooms, looking out onto a palm-shaded swimming pool exclusively for hotel guests.

Breakfast included.

All rooms equipped with private bathroom, hairdryer, air conditioning, TV, telephone, and tea- and coffee-making facilities.

BEACH GARDEN Hotel RATING ★

Perfect for budget travelers, clean and well-kept. Located on the beachfront.

Facilities include: restaurant, coffee shop, swimming pool, tour booking service, laundry service, and guest Internet access.

Water sports and diving equipment available for rent.

Four-bed and six-bed rooms available.

2. Asking for details

Where is the Spa Resort Hotel?	It's on the beach. It's near the center.
Does it have | a swimming pool? | Is there	Yes, it does. / No, it doesn't. Yes, there is. / No, there isn't.
What types of rooms does it have?	It has | double | rooms. | single

PRACTICE

Class CD 2
Track 14

Listen to the example. Use the information in the Practice above to ask and answer questions about the hotels. Student A asks questions about two of the hotels. Reverse roles.

Ask questions about:

1. location   3. facilities   5. tours
2. types of rooms   4. price   6. meals

Use These Words

expensive	cheap
reasonable	comfortable
clean	nice
convenient	friendly

3. Making a reservation

I'd like to reserve a double room at the Spa Resort Hotel, please.	Certainly. For what dates?
From September 23–30.	Could I have your name, please?
Yes, my last name is Park. P-a-r-k.	

PRACTICE

Class CD 2
Track 15

Listen to the example. Student A is a tourist. Student B works in a travel agency. Use the hotels from the Practice in Part 1 to have a conversation. Reverse roles.

LISTEN TO THIS

Class CD 2
Track 16

Part 1 Listen to someone making a reservation at the Palm Tree Hotel. Check (✓) which type of information is mentioned.

____ price

____ type of room

____ location of room

____ meals

____ tours

____ cable TV

Part 2 Listen again and write the name, the dates, and the type of room requested.

Palm Tree Hotel

Name _____

Dates _____

Type of room _____

Part 3 Ask your partner about the things that are available at the Palm Tree Hotel.

Part 1 Work in pairs. Describe your dream hotel by discussing the following questions with your partner. Write your answers.

Where is the hotel?

What is its name?

What kind of rooms does it have?

What kind of facilities does it have?

What kind of tours or trips are available?

How much does it cost to stay there?

Part 2 Work as a class. Interview six students about their hotels using the questions in Part 1. Take turns making reservations at each other's hotels. Write the reservations for your hotel in the chart.

Hotel Reservations			
Person's name	*Type of room*	*From (date)*	*To (date)*

Part 3 Work in groups. Go back to your groups and share the information you learned. How many reservations did you get? Which hotels did you make a reservation at?

Conversation 2
We'd like to check in, please.

Do you often stay in hotels? What kind of room do you prefer?

Class CD 2, Track 17

Julie: We'd like to check in, please.
Clerk: Do you have a reservation?
Julie: Yes, our last names are Park and Kim.
Clerk: Here it is. Could you sign here, please? And I'll need to see your passports.
Julie: Here you are. Do you have a room with an ocean view?
Clerk: Yes, we do. You can have room 43B.
Lisa: And do you know where we can rent some diving gear?
Clerk: You can rent diving equipment from our diving center, just around the corner from the swimming pool. It's open from 7 A.M. to 3 P.M.
Julie: And what time can we get dinner?
Clerk: The restaurant opens for dinner at 6 P.M.
Julie: Thanks.
Clerk: Do you need any help with your bags?
Lisa: No, that's all right. We can manage.

Class CD 2, Track 18
Pronunciation Focus

The verb *can* is usually unstressed. Listen to these sentences.

Do you know where we can rent some diving gear?
What time can we get dinner?
We can manage.

Listen to the conversation again and notice the unstressed examples of *can*.

Student CD, Track 17

1. Checking in

I'd like to check in, please.	Do you have a reservation?
Yes, the last name is Park.	Here it is. Could you sign here, please?

PRACTICE

Class CD 2 Track 19

Listen to the example. Student A is a guest and wants to check in to a hotel. Student B is a desk clerk. Help Student A check in. Reverse roles.

2. Making requests

Do you have	a room with an ocean view?	Yes, certainly. You can have room 43B.
Could I have	a non-smoking room?	I'm sorry. Those rooms are all taken.

PRACTICE

Class CD 2 Track 20

Work in pairs. Listen to the example. Take turns checking in to a hotel. Choose from the list to make your requests. Your partner will use the chart to answer your requests. Reverse roles.

- a room overlooking the pool
- a room far away from the elevators
- a non-smoking room
- a room with an ocean view
- a room with Internet access
- a room near the fitness center

Use These Words

next to
near
facing
overlooking
not far from
far away from
single / double / twin room
suite

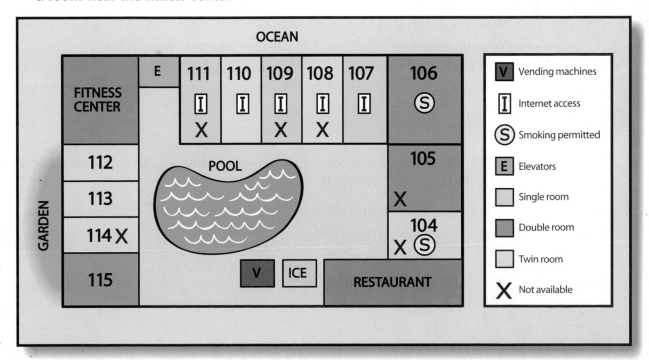

3. Asking about hotel services

Can I help you?	
Could you tell me	what time the restaurant opens for breakfast?
	if you serve breakfast on Sunday?
Yes, of course. Breakfast is served in the restaurant from 7:30 A.M. to 10 A.M.	
Thank you very much.	

PRACTICE

Class CD 2 Track 21

Listen to the example. Student A is a desk clerk. Student B is a hotel guest. Use the information below to have a conversation. Reverse roles.

> ### Hotel Information
>
> **Restaurant:** Breakfast 7:30 – 10:00 A.M.
> Lunch 11:30 A.M. – 2:00 P.M.
> Dinner 6:00 – 11:30 P.M.
>
> **Fitness center:** Swimming pool and sauna 5:30 A.M. – 4:00 P.M.
> Exercise room: 9:00 A.M. – 4:00 P.M.
>
> **Business center:** Conference facilities available for groups.
> Fax and Internet access for individuals on request, $16 per hour.
>
> **Wake-up calls:** Automated wake-up calls available on request.
>
> *Limousine service to the airport and for city tours. Reservations at front desk.*

1. What time is breakfast?
2. When is the pool open?
3. Where can I send a fax?
4. Can I get a wake-up call?
5. Can I send an e-mail?
6. What kind of facilities does the fitness center have?
7. Can I get a limo to the airport?
8. Do you arrange any tours?

LISTEN TO THIS

Class CD 2 Track 22

Part 1 Listen to three conversations between a hotel guest and a desk clerk. Write the guest's request in the chart.

Part 2 Listen again and write the name and room number of each person.

	Request	Name	Room number
1			
2			
3			

Part 3 Were the requests successful or not?

(Student A looks at this page. Student B looks at page 111.)

Part 1 Read the hotel brochure. Ask your partner questions to fill in the missing information.

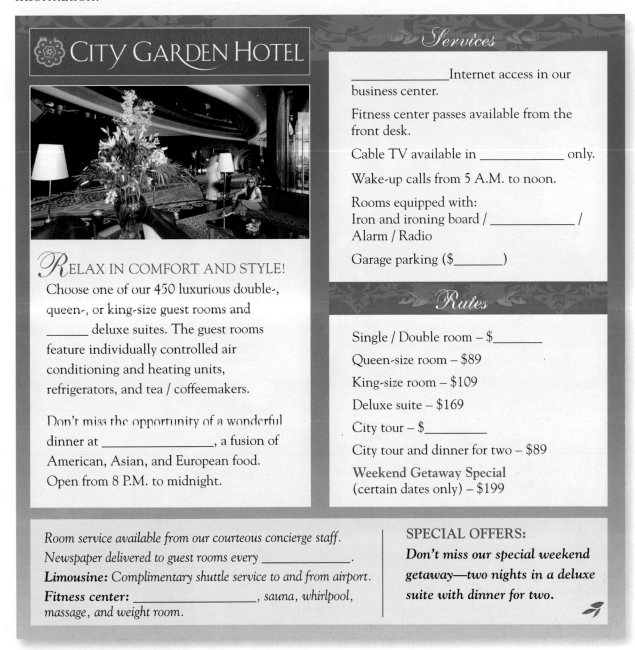

City Garden Hotel

*R*ELAX IN COMFORT AND STYLE!
Choose one of our 450 luxurious double-, queen-, or king-size guest rooms and _____ deluxe suites. The guest rooms feature individually controlled air conditioning and heating units, refrigerators, and tea / coffeemakers.

Don't miss the opportunity of a wonderful dinner at _____, a fusion of American, Asian, and European food. Open from 8 P.M. to midnight.

Services

_____ Internet access in our business center.

Fitness center passes available from the front desk.

Cable TV available in _____ only.

Wake-up calls from 5 A.M. to noon.

Rooms equipped with:
Iron and ironing board / _____ / Alarm / Radio

Garage parking ($_____)

Rules

Single / Double room – $_____
Queen-size room – $89
King-size room – $109
Deluxe suite – $169
City tour – $_____
City tour and dinner for two – $89
Weekend Getaway Special
(certain dates only) – $199

Room service available from our courteous concierge staff.
Newspaper delivered to guest rooms every _____.
***Limousine:** Complimentary shuttle service to and from airport.*
***Fitness center:** _____, sauna, whirlpool, massage, and weight room.*

SPECIAL OFFERS:
Don't miss our special weekend getaway—two nights in a deluxe suite with dinner for two.

Part 2 Now answer your partner's questions about the hotel brochure.

Part 3 You are a tourist. Call the hotel to make a reservation. Ask about hotel services and facilities. Say what kind of room you would like, and give the dates and your name. Use the brochure above.

Now Try This

Describe your dream hotel. Tell your partner about it and answer his or her questions.

Do you plan your trips carefully or do you decide what to do when you get there?

Class CD 2, Track 23

Sang-woo: Hi. Can you help me? I'm here for a week and I need some ideas for things to do.

Guide: I have some brochures here. What are you interested in seeing here in Hong Kong?

Sang-woo: First, I want to see the famous sights.

Guide: Of course, you shouldn't miss Victoria Peak. You take a cable car to the top, and you can get fantastic views of the city from there.

Sang-woo: That's a good idea. What else is there to do?

Guide: Hundreds of things! If you like shopping, there are lots of street markets where you can get really good bargains on clothing, antiques...whatever you like.

Sang-woo: I'm not really interested in that. What's there to do at night?

Guide: There are clubs, concerts, plays...you name it.

Sang-woo: That sounds exciting!

Student CD, Track 18

1. Getting information

I need some ideas for things to do in Hong Kong.	What are you interested in seeing? What do you want to see?
First, I want to see the famous sights.	You shouldn't miss Victoria Peak. You can get fantastic views from there. Then you can go shopping.

PRACTICE 1

Class CD 2 Track 24

Listen to the example. Student A is a guide in Hong Kong. Student B is a tourist. Use the information below to have a conversation.

1. Victoria Peak—fantastic views of the city
2. Floating restaurants—fresh seafood and views of the bay
3. Street markets—amazing bargains
4. Temples—wish for good luck and find out your fortune

PRACTICE 2

Reverse roles. Student B is a guide in Singapore. Student A is a tourist. Use the information below to have a conversation.

1. Old Chinatown—stores, old houses, and temples
2. Jurong Bird Park—tropical birds fly freely under a forest canopy
3. The Raffles Hotel—old-fashioned style and elegance
4. Sentosa Island—beaches, nature trails, and more

2. Discussing possible activities

What is there to do?	
If you like shopping,	there are lots of street markets. you can get really good bargains at the street markets. you should visit the street markets.
That's a good idea. I'm not really interested in that. What else is there to do?	

PRACTICE 1

Class CD 2 Track 25

Listen to the example. Then take turns asking your partner about activities in Hong Kong or Singapore. Use the cues below, and the pictures and information on the previous page.

1. birdwatching
2. animals
3. shopping
4. hiking

5. swimming
6. eating out
7. historic buildings
8. taking pictures

Use These Words

diving   sunbathing
sight-seeing   snorkeling
climbing   exploring
relaxing   browsing

PRACTICE 2

Your partner is planning his or her next vacation. Find out what he or she is interested in and recommend one of these places. Say what you can do there. Reverse roles.

Fiji

Italy

Kenya

LISTEN TO THIS

Class CD 2 Track 26

Part 1 Listen to descriptions of two places. Write the name of each place in the chart.

Part 2 Listen again and write what you can see and do in each place.

	Place	Things to see and do
1		
2		

Part 3 Which place would be good for a family to visit on vacation? Why?

Part 1 Think of three things you like to do on vacation. Write them in the chart.

Your interests	Places you could go

Part 2 Walk around the class and ask your classmates for advice about where to go for your next vacation. Write the names of the places that match your interests in the chart.

Part 3 How many places did you find? Which place would you choose?

Part 4 Work in pairs. What things are most important to you when choosing a vacation destination? Make a list of the top five things. Compare your lists with the class.

Conversation 2
How do I get there?

How do you find your way around a new city?

Sang-woo: What's the best way to get to Waterfront Park from here? Can I take the subway?

Guide: No, but you can catch the number 34 bus in front of that hotel. Get off at Harbor Street. Actually, it's just a short walk from here.

Sang-woo: Really? How far is it?

Guide: About ten or fifteen minutes. You know, there are also guided tours of the city you can take.

Sang-woo: Oh? What does the city tour include?

Guide: They take you around the major points of interest. You can get a good idea of where everything is.

Sang-woo: Hmm. How much is it?

Guide: It's $10.00 per person for a one-hour tour. The tour bus stops across the street from here, and there should be one in about ten minutes. You can buy a ticket on the bus.

Sang-woo: Thanks. That sounds like a great idea.

Pronunciation Focus

Words ending in a [t] sound are often linked to words beginning with a vowel. Listen and practice these phrases.

front of   get off
just a   get a

Listen to the conversation again and notice the linked words.

1. Asking about public transportation

Excuse me.	What's the best way to get to How do I get to	Waterfront Park from here? Can I take	a bus? the subway?
Yes, you	can catch the number 34 bus. take the subway to the Museum Station. Take the Green Line to Museum. Then change to the Red Line. Get off at Baker.		
Oh, it's just a short walk from here.			
Actually, it's best to take a taxi from here.			

PRACTICE 1

**Class CD 2
Track 29**

Listen to the example. Then ask your partner about getting to four of the following places by public transportation. Use the information in the box to answer. Reverse roles.

1. Harper's Bay Mall
2. Opera House
3. Sports Stadium
4. Strand Theater
5. Central Park
6. Lakeshore Zoo
7. Mercy Hospital
8. Farmers' Market

**Take City Transit!
Cheaper, Faster, More Convenient**

Bus Routes		Subway Stations	
Sports Stadium	#67	Strand Theater	Baker
Harper's Bay Mall	#52	Central Park	Main
Lakeshore Zoo	#17	Opera House	King
Olde Towne	#14	Mercy Hospital	College
The Docks	#14	Farmers' Market	Market

PRACTICE 2

Use the subway map below to ask and answer questions about how to get to the stations in Practice 1 from Grand Station.

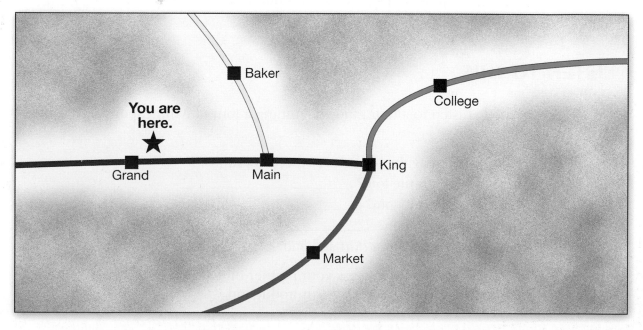

2. Talking about tours

What does the city tour include? Where does the bus tour go?	It's a guided bus tour of They take you around	the entire city. the major points of interest.
How much is it? does it cost?	It's $10.00 per person for a	one-hour tour. two-hour
Is lunch provided?	Yes, it is.	

PRACTICE 1

Class CD 2 Track 30

Listen to the example. Student A asks his or her partner questions to get all the details about the walking tour. Student B uses the information below to answer.

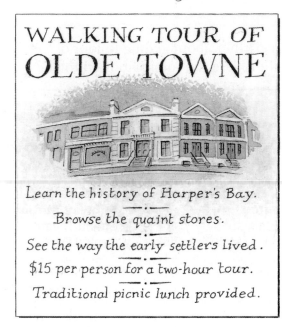

WALKING TOUR OF OLDE TOWNE

Learn the history of Harper's Bay.

Browse the quaint stores.

See the way the early settlers lived.

$15 per person for a two-hour tour.

Traditional picnic lunch provided.

Harper's Bay HARBOR TOUR

View Olde Towne and downtown from the harbor and relax aboard the MINNOW.

$20 PER PERSON for a 3-hour tour (includes buffet lunch).

PRACTICE 2

Student B asks his or her partner questions to get all the details about the harbor tour. Student A uses the information above to answer.

Use These Words

start from	picturesque
get off	comfortable
finish	fascinating
get on	memorable

LISTEN TO THIS

Class CD 2 Track 31

Part 1 Listen to a tour guide beginning a tour of Minneapolis. What kind of tour is it?

Part 2 Listen again and answer these questions.
1. How much is the tour? _____
2. How long is the tour? _____
3. How long is lunch? _____
4. Where does the tour start and end? _____

Part 3 Listen again and ask your partner three more questions about the information in the tour guide's introduction.

(Student A looks at this page. Student B looks at page 112.)

Part 1 Read the information about Vancouver, Canada. Which places are good for what kind of interests?

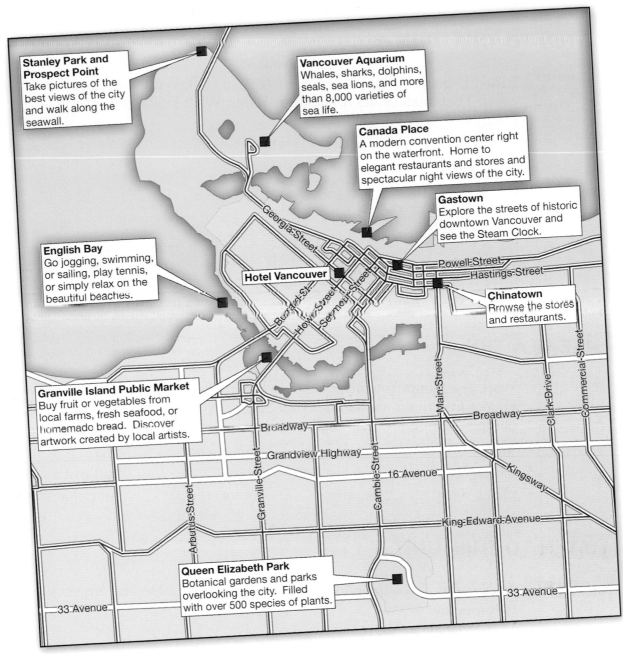

Stanley Park and Prospect Point
Take pictures of the best views of the city and walk along the seawall.

Vancouver Aquarium
Whales, sharks, dolphins, seals, sea lions, and more than 8,000 varieties of sea life.

Canada Place
A modern convention center right on the waterfront. Home to elegant restaurants and stores and spectacular night views of the city.

Gastown
Explore the streets of historic downtown Vancouver and see the Steam Clock.

English Bay
Go jogging, swimming, or sailing, play tennis, or simply relax on the beautiful beaches.

Hotel Vancouver

Chinatown
Browse the stores and restaurants.

Granville Island Public Market
Buy fruit or vegetables from local farms, fresh seafood, or homemade bread. Discover artwork created by local artists.

Queen Elizabeth Park
Botanical gardens and parks overlooking the city. Filled with over 500 species of plants.

Georgia Street, Burrard St., Howe Street, Seymour Street, Powell Street, Hastings Street, Main Street, Clark Drive, Commercial Street, Broadway, Grandview Highway, Gamble Street, 16 Avenue, Kingsway, King Edward Avenue, Arbutus Street, Granville Street, 33 Avenue, 33 Avenue

Part 2 You are a tour guide. Your partner is a tourist visiting Vancouver for one day. Help your partner decide which sights he or she wants to visit and explain how to get there from the Hotel Vancouver.

Part 3 Your partner is only visiting Vancouver for one day. What places should he or she definitely visit? Why? Compare your answers with your partner.

Now Try This

Choose another town or city that you know. Give your partner advice about what to see and do there.

Review:
Units 7–9

LISTEN TO THIS UNIT 7

Class CD 2
Track 32

Listen to the instructions on how to make a craft. Write down the things you will need. Then make notes of the instructions. What kind of object is it?

Tools	Instructions	
	Step 1	
	Step 2	
	Step 3	
	Step 4	
	Step 5	
	Step 6	

GIVE IT A TRY

Work as a group. You are going to live on a desert island for a year. In your group, choose five things to take with you. Say why you will need each item. Then compare your choices with other groups.

string	compass	sleeping bag	knife
flashlight	matches	whistle	bottle of aspirin
plastic sheet	hammer	mirror	tube of antiseptic cream

LISTEN TO THIS UNIT 8

Class CD 2
Track 33

A woman is checking in to the Shamrock Motel. Listen and answer the following questions.

1. How much are the rooms? _____

2. Put a check (✓) beside the things that are available.

☐ swimming pool   ☐ vending machines

☐ fitness center   ☐ gift shop

☐ restaurant   ☐ wake-up calls

☐ coffee shop   ☐ cable TV

GIVE IT A TRY

Think of your dream hotel. Write the information in the chart below. Then find out about your partner's hotel. Write the information in the chart and practice making a reservation.

Your hotel

Hotel name _____
Location _____
Types of accommodation
_____
_____
Rates _____
Facilities _____
Tours or trips _____
Special offers _____

Your partner's hotel

Hotel name _____
Location _____
Types of accommodation
_____
_____
Rates _____
Facilities _____
Tours or trips _____
Special offers _____

LISTEN TO THIS UNIT 9

Class CD 2
Track 34

You are going to hear a description of a London bus tour. Listen and write the information in the chart.

What do you see?	Cost / Time	What's included?	What's not included?

GIVE IT A TRY

Part 1 Work as a group. In your group, plan a tour of your town or neighborhood. First, choose four places that you think a visitor should see and discuss why tourists should go there. Take notes below.

Place 1: _____	Place 2: _____	Place 3: _____	Place 4: _____

Part 2 Find a partner from another group. You are a tourist. Your partner is a tour guide. Have a conversation using the notes from your chart. Then reverse roles. Who gave the best advice?

Conversation 1
Who's that woman?

Describe the people in the picture. What words or phrases did you use?

Class CD 2, Track 35

Mariko: I've been here nearly six months, and I still don't know half the people here. Who's that woman?

Bob: Where?

Mariko: The one in the purple sweater.

Bob: I don't know. I never saw her before. Why?

Mariko: I think she's the one who just moved into my apartment building.

Bob: Oh, yeah?

Mariko: And do you know who that man is?

Bob: Which one?

Mariko: The one in the blue jacket. I think I've met him before.

Bob: That's Matt Chang.

Mariko: Is he the one whose brother drives the red sports car?

Bob: Yeah, that's right.

Mariko: Well, Matt's the one I'd like to meet. Can you introduce me to him?

Student CD, Track 20

1. Asking who someone is

Who's that woman? Do you know who that man / guy is?		Which one?				
The one	in the purple sweater. in the blue jacket. next to the telephone.	I have no idea. I'm not sure.	I never saw	her him	before.
		I think she / he is the one who just moved into my apartment building.				

PRACTICE 1

**Class CD 2
Track 36**

Listen to the example. Take turns asking and answering questions about the people below.

- works at the Mexican Embassy
- is a sports reporter
- moved into the house next door

- opened a new Korean restaurant
- won a music scholarship
- teaches French at the high school

PRACTICE 2

Ask your partner questions about other people in the room. Use your own ideas to answer.

2. Identifying someone

| Is Matt (he) the one whose brother drives the red sports car? | Yes, that's right. No. His brother drives a motorcycle. |

| Is he the one whose girlfriend sings in a rock band? | No. His girlfriend plays the guitar. |

PRACTICE 1

Class CD 2
Track 37

Listen to the example. Student A asks about three guests at a party. Student B confirms or corrects Student A's guesses. Use the information below to have a conversation. Reverse roles and talk about the other three people.

1 Alex / sister owns a music store

2 Anna / sister just got married

3 Tom / son plays guitar in a band

4 Yoshi and Chie / dog had puppies

5 Arthur / daughter is a dancer

6 Jan / brother designs websites

PRACTICE 2

Make guesses about other students in the class. Your partner will confirm or correct your information. Follow the model from Practice 1. Reverse roles.

LISTEN TO THIS

Class CD 2
Track 38

Part 1 Listen to two people talking about people at a party. Write the names of the three people they are talking about.

Part 2 Listen again and write the information about each person.

Part 3 Think of a question to ask each of the three people at the party.

Name	Information

LET'S TALK

Part 1 Work in groups. Choose one person to be the secretary. Each person in the group will think of one unusual or interesting fact about themselves. The secretary will write the facts on a piece of paper like this:

> I went to Australia on vacation last winter.
> My favorite sport is in-line skating.
> I love video games.
> My sister is a chess champion.
> My brother is in a rock band.

Part 2 Work in groups. Exchange papers with another group. Talk about the facts on the paper. Who does each fact belong to? Have the secretary write the group's guesses.

Part 3 When your group has finished, check your answers with the other group.

Part 4 Repeat the activity with the other groups in the class.

Conversation 2
What's she like?

Think of the best and the worst teacher you have ever had. Why was he or she so good or bad?

Class CD 2, Track 39

Mariko: Hi, Rosa. What are you doing?

Rosa: I'm trying to pick an English literature class for this semester.

Mariko: Take Professor Holt's class. I had her last year.

Rosa: Really? What's she like?

Mariko: Fantastic! I think she's a great teacher.

Rosa: Why? What makes her so great?

Mariko: For one thing, she's really funny.

Rosa: Yeah, but I want to learn something.

Mariko: Don't get me wrong. She's funny, and if someone's funny, you pay more attention. She's also really smart, so you learn a lot.

Rosa: What do you think of Professor Vance?

Mariko: He's boring. Everyone falls asleep in his class. And he's not very easy to talk to.

Rosa: OK. I'll try to take Professor Holt's class.

Mariko: I'm sure you'll enjoy it!

Student CD, Track 21

Class CD 2, Track 40
Pronunciation Focus

Listen to the [r] sound after a vowel in these words.

learn	literature
smart	professor
year	teacher

Listen to the conversation again and notice the words with an [r] sound after a vowel.

1. Asking what someone is like

What's he / she like?	He's really funny.
What do you think of Professor Vance?	He's boring.
	He's not very easy to talk to.

PRACTICE 1

Look at the vocabulary below. Decide with your partner if the qualities listed below are positive or negative and write them in the chart. Think of more adjectives and add them to the list. Compare your lists with your classmates'.

outgoing
smart
aggressive
greedy
strict
open-minded
stingy
considerate
honest
conceited
moody
hardworking

Positive qualities	Negative qualities

PRACTICE 2

Class CD 2 Track 41

Listen to the example. Think of a famous entertainer or athlete and write the name below. Write four adjectives to describe what you think he or she is like. Then ask two classmates. Write their answers in the chart. Discuss your results in a group.

Entertainer's or athlete's name: _____	
Your opinion	
Classmate 1	
Classmate 2	

Use These Words

really	pretty
very	quite
kind of	a bit
a little	not very

2. Discussing qualities

What makes her so great?	She's funny. If someone's funny, you pay more attention. She's smart, so you can learn a lot from her.

PRACTICE 1

Think of four people you like. Check (✓) the words from the vocabulary list below that describe them.

- ☐ calm
- ☐ polite
- ☐ practical
- ☐ confident
- ☐ brave
- ☐ supportive
- ☐ sensitive
- ☐ reliable
- ☐ generous
- ☐ friendly
- ☐ hardworking
- ☐ nervous

PRACTICE 2

Class CD 2 Track 42

Work in pairs. Listen to the example. Discusss the people and their qualities that you chose in Practice 1. Reverse roles.

LISTEN TO THIS

Class CD 2 Track 43

Part 1 Listen to a boy and a girl discussing a birthday gift. What was the gift, and why was the boy unhappy about it?

Part 2 What adjectives could you use to describe the boy's and the girl's personalities?

	Adjectives
Boy	
Girl	

Part 3 Which of these adjectives are positive? Which are negative? Which adjectives could have both positive and negative meanings?

(Student A looks at this page. Student B looks at page 113.)

Part 1 Read the following statements spoken by different people. What kind of person do you think said each statement? Write the adjective next to each one.

conceited   confident   outgoing   shy   argumentative
supportive   greedy   kind   rude   hardworking

When I go to a party,…	Adjective
1. I try to talk to as many people as I can.	
2. I feel sure when I talk to others.	
3. I try to help people make friends with each other.	
4. I offer to help people with their problems.	
5. My friends usually ask me to help clean up after the party.	
6. I usually talk to people I already know.	
7. I tell people about how successful I am.	
8. I often get into arguments with people who don't agree with me.	
9. I try to get as much free food and drinks as I can.	
10. I ignore people I don't like.	

Part 2 Your partner has different statements. Take turns reading the statements aloud and match the ones you think were said by the same people.

Part 3 Look at the list of jobs below. Your partner has a different list of jobs. Decide which person above is right for each job.

doctor

lawyer

teacher

nurse

police officer

Now Try This

Which statements in Part 1 are true for you? Tell your partner. Ask for advice about which job would be good for you.

Conversation 1
Have you ever tried it?

What kind of sports equipment can you see in the picture? What kind of sports do you like?

Who was the first skysurfer?
Joel Cruciani from France
When was his first jump?
1987
How fast do skysurfers fall?
Up to 150 kilometers per hour!
What do you need for skysurfing?
skyboard ($800); jumpsuit ($500); parachute ($3,000); certification ($2,500)

● Would you like to skysurf?

Class CD 2, Track 44

Max:	Look at this equipment! I think there's something for every winter sport here.
Shigeo:	I'll say! Look at this snowboarding gear. Have you ever tried snowboarding?
Max:	Snowboarding? No, I've never done it. Have you?
Shigeo:	I tried it once.
Max:	You're kidding. When?
Shigeo:	Last year when I went to Korea.
Max:	What was it like? Was it fun?
Shigeo:	Oh, yeah. I fell down a lot at first. But it was really cool.
Max:	Did you try any other sports there?
Shigeo:	Yeah, we did some rock climbing. Have you ever done that?
Max:	Lots of times. I used to go every weekend. The last time was in the spring. I fell and hurt my leg.
Shigeo:	That's too bad. How about bungee-jumping? That's really scary.
Max:	Now that's something I *don't* want to try!

Student CD, Track 22

1. Discussing experiences (1)

Have you ever tried snowboarding?	No, I've never done it. Have you?
Yes, I have.	When?
I've done it lots of times. I tried it last year. I go snowboarding every weekend.	

PRACTICE 1

Class CD 2
Track 45

Listen to the example. Then ask your partner if he or she has done any of the following things. Reverse roles.

① mountain biking   ② skateboarding   ③ cross-country skiing

④ whitewater rafting   ⑤ hang gliding   ⑥ bungee-jumping

PRACTICE 2

If your partner answered yes to any of the things in Practice 1, find out when your partner did them.

2. Discussing experiences (2)

When was the last time you went mountain climbing?
The last time was in the spring. I fell and hurt my leg.

PRACTICE

Class CD 2
Track 46

Listen to the example. Then ask your partner about the last time he or she did any of the following things. Reverse roles.

1. went swimming
2. went skiing
3. rode a bike
4. played table tennis

5. did tai chi
6. played baseball
7. went jogging
8. your idea _____

3. Discussing experiences (3)

What was it like?	I was	terrified at first.
Was it fun?		really scared.
Did you like it?	It was	really exciting.
		a lot of fun.
	I loved it. / I hated it.	

Use These Words

I felt...	It was...
scared	scary
terrified	terrifying
excited	exciting
interested	interesting
bored	boring
disappointed	disappointing
frustrated	frustrating
tired	tiring

PRACTICE 1

Class CD 2 Track 47

Listen to the example. Then tell your partner about an interesting sport or activity you have tried. Your partner will ask how you felt about it. Reverse roles.

PRACTICE 2

Write the names of three sports in each category below. Find out if your partner agrees. Explain the reasons for your choices.

exciting	dangerous	boring	terrifying

LISTEN TO THIS

Class CD 2 Track 48

Part 1 Listen to three people talking about different sports they have tried. Number the pictures in the correct order.

Part 2 Listen again and write the key words that helped you identify each sport.

Part 3 How did each person feel? How did they describe the experience?

Part 1 In the chart, write five sports you have tried and when you last did each one. Then write one adjective that you think describes each sport.

Sport	You		Classmate 1	Classmate 2	Classmate 3
	When:		When:	When:	When:
	Opinion:		Opinion:	Opinion:	Opinion:
	When:		When:	When:	When:
	Opinion:		Opinion:	Opinion:	Opinion:
	When:		When:	When:	When:
	Opinion:		Opinion:	Opinion:	Opinion:
	When:		When:	When:	When:
	Opinion:		Opinion:	Opinion:	Opinion:
	When:		When:	When:	When:
	Opinion:		Opinion:	Opinion:	Opinion:

Part 2 Walk around the class and find other classmates who have tried the same sports. When did they try the sport? What did they think of it? Write their answers in the chart.

Part 3 Would you recommend the sports you wrote in the chart? Tell the class why or why not. Which sport was the most popular?

Conversation 2
I'll never forget the time I...

Think of an experience you had that you'll never forget. Why do you think you remember it so well?

Class CD 2, Track 49

Shigeo: Did I ever tell you about the time I found some money on the train?

Max: No. What happened?

Shigeo: I was taking the train to my judo class, when I saw a wallet on the seat next to me. I picked it up, and it had about $150 in it.

Max: What did you do? Did you keep the money?

Shigeo: No. I handed it to a police officer when I got off.

Max: Good for you. That was really honest of you.

Shigeo: I had a nice surprise three months later. They called me and gave me the money. They couldn't find the person who lost it.

Max: Well, I'll never forget the time I lost money.

Shigeo: Oh, no. Was it a lot?

Max: I was on the train when I realized I had forgotten my train pass. I took out my wallet to pay for the ticket and my wallet was empty! I was sure I had about $100.

Shigeo: So what did you do about the ticket? How did you get home?

Max: Oh, I had to get out at the next station and walk! I went home and I searched everywhere.

Shigeo: Did you ever find it?

Max: You won't believe it. I found it the next time I did laundry. It was in my pants' pocket the whole time.

Student CD, Track 23

Class CD 2, Track 50
Pronunciation Focus

Listen to the final *-ed* sound in these words.

[t]	[d]	[id]
picked	called	handed

Listen to the conversation again and notice the final *-ed* sound.

1. Telling a story

Did I ever tell you Have I ever told you	about the time I found $150?	No. What happened?
I was taking the train to my judo class, when I saw a wallet on the seat next to me.		What did you do?
I gave it to a police officer when I got off.		

PRACTICE 1

Class CD 2 Track 51

Listen to the example. Student A chooses one of the pictures below and tells Student B his or her story. Student B asks questions to get more details. Reverse roles.

broke my leg

locked myself out

helped a hurt child

met a famous person

PRACTICE 2

Class CD 2 Track 52

Listen to the example. Then think about what happened next in each story. Take turns telling the story again and continue as long as possible by asking questions.

PRACTICE 3

Tell your partner about an unusual experience you have had, or choose one of the situations below. Your partner will ask questions to get more details. Reverse roles.

1. the worst thing you did as a child
2. the bravest thing you ever did
3. the most embarrassing moment of your life
4. the best vacation you ever had
5. your idea _____

2. Responding to someone's story

| I turned the wallet in to the police. | Good for you. That was really honest of you. Did they find the owner? |

| I lost some money. | Oh, no. That's terrible. Was it a lot? Did you find it? |

PRACTICE

Class CD 2
Track 53

Listen to the example. Tell your partner about an experience you will never forget, or choose one of the ideas below. Your partner will respond and ask questions to get more details. Reverse roles.

- a time you found or lost something valuable
- a time when you helped someone
- a time when someone helped you
- your idea _____

Use These Words

Oh, that's too bad!
That's terrible!
I'm happy to hear that!
Great!
That's unbelievable!
Incredible!
Amazing!
I can't believe it!

LISTEN TO THIS

Class CD 2
Track 54

Part 1 Listen to Lisa's story. Think of a good title for the story and write it below.
Title: _____

Part 2 How did the Lisa feel at each stage of the story? Write adjectives under each picture.

_____   _____   _____

_____   _____   _____

Part 3 Listen again and ask your partner three questions about what happened in the story.

Part 1 Think of an unusual event or story that happened to you and write down some notes about it.

What happened? _____

Where did it happen? _____

When did it happen? _____

What were you doing? _____

What did you do next? _____

How did you feel? _____

Part 2 Work in groups. In your group, decide who will be Students A, B, C, and D. Students A and B will share their stories with each other. Students C and D will share theirs. Take notes about your partner's story.

Part 3 Work with a new partner in your group. Tell the story you just heard to your new partner. Take notes.

Now Try This

Work in the same groups. Each person tells the last story they heard to the whole group. The others listen carefully and ask questions. The person who told the original story will check that the information is correct.

Conversation 1
What did you think of it?

How often do you watch movies? What makes you decide to go and see a movie?

Class CD 2, Track 55

Angie:	What did you think of the movie?
John:	I thought it was great.
Angie:	You did? I thought it was terrible.
John:	Why? What didn't you like about it?
Angie:	For one thing, it was too violent. There was too much fighting.
John:	But, Angie, it was a martial arts movie!
Angie:	I know, but the story was silly, too.
John:	The stories are always silly in those movies.
Angie:	Then why do you like them?
John:	They're exciting and I like the fight scenes.
Angie:	Yeah, but the acting is terrible.
John:	They don't have to act. They just have to know how to fight. It's like watching a dance.
Angie:	Then maybe we should go to the ballet next time!

Student CD, Track 24

GIVE IT A TRY

1. Asking and giving opinions

What did you think of Did you like	the movie? the TV show? the game? the concert?	I thought it was great. I loved it. I thought it was so-so. It wasn't bad. I thought it was terrible. I hated it.

PRACTICE

Class CD 2 Track 56

Listen to the example. Take turns asking and answering questions about three of the events below.

1. last weekend's new movies
2. the last Jackie Chan movie
3. the last music CD you bought
4. last night's TV programs
5. the last concert you went to
6. last weekend's sports events

2. Agreeing and disagreeing with opinions

I loved it.	So did I.

I thought it was great.	So did I. I thought it was good, too. I thought so, too. You did? I thought it was terrible.

I didn't like it at all. I didn't think it was very good.	Neither did I. I didn't like it either. I didn't think so either. You didn't? I loved it.

PRACTICE 1

Class CD 2 Track 57

Listen to the example. Then think of a recent well-known example for each of the following and write it below. Take turns asking for each other's opinions. Remember to agree or disagree.

Student A
1. a movie _____
2. a TV show _____
3. a music CD _____

Student B
1. a book _____
2. a sports event _____
3. a new music video _____

PRACTICE 2

Walk around the room and ask other classmates' opinions about the items in Practice 1. Agree or disagree with them.

3. Giving reasons

What didn't you like about it? Why didn't you like it?	It was too violent. The story was silly.

What did you like about it? Why did you like it?	It was exciting. The acting was excellent.

PRACTICE 1

Class CD 2
Track 58

Listen to the example. Then decide on a movie that you and your partner have both seen. Find out what your partner thought of it. Give reasons for your opinions by talking about the ideas below.

1. the acting
2. the story
3. the characters
4. the special effects
5. the soundtrack
6. the ending

Use These Words

happy	depressing
interesting	confusing
realistic	boring
funny	scary
fast-paced	slow-moving

PRACTICE 2

Talk with your partner about a TV show that you have both seen. Find out what your partner thought of it. Talk about the story, the characters, and the acting.

PRACTICE 3

Talk with your partner about a book that you have both read. Find out what your partner thought of it. Talk about the story, the characters, the writing style, and the ending.

LISTEN TO THIS

Class CD 2
Track 59

Part 1 Listen to two movie critics discussing a movie. Write a check (✔) if the speaker liked the following things. Write an (✗) if he or she didn't.

Part 2 Listen again and write down the reasons why the critics liked or didn't like each thing.

	✔ / ✗	Jean's Reasons	✔ / ✗	Henry's Reasons
Story				
Characters				
Acting				

Part 3 Did the critics recommend the movie or not?

Part 1 Work in groups. Write the titles of four movies that everyone in your group has seen.

1. _____

2. _____

3. _____

4. _____

Part 2 For each movie, write your opinions about each category in the chart. Then give each movie a score.

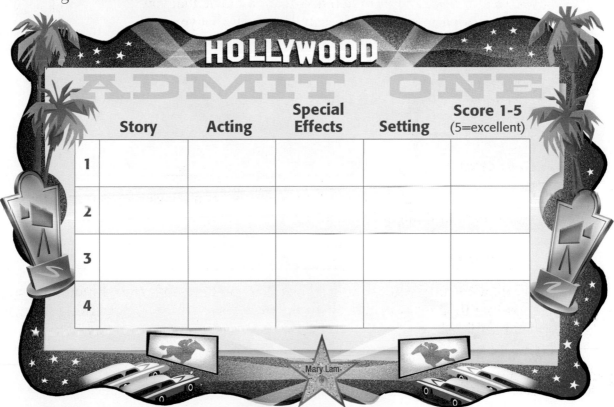

	Story	Acting	Special Effects	Setting	Score 1-5 (5=excellent)
1					
2					
3					
4					

Part 3 Work in groups. Discuss your opinions with your group. Discuss each category. Then vote on the movies. Which movie is the most popular?

Part 4 Write your group's winning movie on the board. One person from each group will tell the class why that movie was the best. When all the groups are finished, vote on the best movie.

Conversation 2
If you ask me...

Do you think violence in movies can be harmful?
Does it cause people to be violent?

Class CD 2, Track 60

Angie: That movie was so violent—it was hard for me to sit through it! What do you think about violence in movies? Do you think it's harmful?

John: I don't think violence in movies is that bad.

Angie: Well, if you ask me, I think it is a problem. Kids grow up thinking that it's OK to hurt people.

John: Oh, come on! I think people worry too much about violence on TV and in the movies. It's not something kids take seriously. I don't think it affects their behavior.

Angie: Oh, no? Then why is it that kids nowadays are so aggressive and have so many social problems in school?

John: Well, personally, I think romantic movies with happy endings are silly. They give people unrealistic expectations.

Angie: That's true. They are superficial and they don't deal with real-life issues at all. But at least they don't encourage people to commit crimes and kill each other.

Class CD 2, Track 61
Pronunciation Focus

Listen to the soft and hard [th] sounds in these words.

through	that
think	they
something	then

Listen to the conversation again and notice the two [th] sounds.

Student CD, Track 25

1. Asking and giving opinions

What do you think about What is your opinion about How do you feel about	violence in movies? romantic movies?	Well, if you ask me, I think it is a problem. Kids grow up thinking that it's OK to hurt people. Personally, I think romantic movies with happy endings are silly. They give people unrealistic expectations.
I think so, too. I agree. You're absolutely right. I don't know about that. I don't think so. Sorry, but I disagree.		

PRACTICE

Class CD 2
Track 62

Listen to the example. Then choose a type of TV show and ask your partner for his or her opinion. Agree or disagree with your partner and give a reason why. Reverse roles.

1. police / crime shows
2. sports programs
3. comedies
4. game shows
5. the news

6. science programs
7. commercials
8. cartoons
9. dramas
10. your idea _____

Use These Words

waste of time	entertaining
one-sided	creative
unrealistic	educational

2. Agreeing and adding a reason

Personally, I think romantic movies with happy endings are silly. They give people unrealistic expectations.
That's true. They're so superficial. They don't deal with real-life issues at all.

PRACTICE

Class CD 2
Track 63

Listen to the example. Then take turns giving your opinion about each of the topics below and giving a reason. Your partner will agree and give an additional reason. Reverse roles.

1. video games
2. the Internet
3. school
4. soccer
5. rap music
6. your idea _____

3. Seeing the other side

> I think romantic movies with happy endings are silly. They give people unrealistic expectations.
>
> That's true, but at least they don't encourage people to commit crimes and kill each other. That's true, but…
>
> Oh come on! Everyone knows they're not real.

PRACTICE

Class CD 2
Track 64

Listen to the example. Then take turns giving your opinion about each of the topics below and giving a reason. Your partner will disagree and give an opposite opinion. Reverse roles.

LISTEN TO THIS

Class CD 2
Track 65

Part 1 Listen to two conversations. In each one, a man and a woman are discussing a social issue. Write down the topic of each conversation.

Part 2 Listen again and write down who is for and who is against each topic, and the reason why.

	Topic	Man's opinion	Woman's opinion
1			
2			

Part 3 Can you think of any additional arguments for or against each topic?

(Student A looks at this page. Student B looks at page 114.)

Part 1 Read the survey on the topic of learning English. Write A if you agree, or D if you disagree.

Questionnaire
about Listening Skills in English

		You	Your Partner
1	Listening to English is easier than reading it.		
2	The most difficult thing about listening to English is the pronunciation.		
3	If I can't understand all the words, I start to feel anxious.		
4	When I listen to someone speaking, I find it difficult to respond immediately.		
5	When I listen to English, it is quite easy to pick out the main ideas.		
6	Asking questions helps me understand what someone is saying.		
7	Listening to the TV or radio needs different skills from listening to someone speaking.		
8	Learning in a group helps me improve my listening skills.		

What advice would you give to someone just starting to learn English on how to improve their listening skills?

Part 2 Interview Student B. Ask for reasons for his or her opinions. Make notes about your partner's reasons. Agree or disagree and respond with your own reasons. Reverse roles. Student B will interview you about learning English. Give reasons for your opinions.

Part 3 Use the notes about your partner's reasons to report to the class on your interview. Summarize your partner's opinions.

Now Try This

Work in pairs. Choose another topic in your school and make up a survey. Exchange surveys with another pair and interview them. Then report to the class.

Review:
Units 10–12

**Class CD 2
Track 66**

Listen to three conversations. Which of these characteristics best describes each person? (You can use more than one adjective for each person.)

aggressive	conceited	confident	considerate	friendly
kind	moody	outgoing	polite	rude
sensitive	shy	stingy	stubborn	supportive

	Man	**Woman**
1		
2		
3		

GIVE IT A TRY

Work in pairs. Look at the people on page 81. Student A chooses one of the people in the pictures. Student B guesses which person Student A chose by asking questions. Reverse roles.
Example:
Is he or she the one who…?

**Class CD 2
Track 67**

Listen to Joshua describing a strange experience. Make notes about the main points of the story. Then with your partner, think of a newspaper headline for the story.

1. When did it happen?	
2. What was he doing?	
3. What did he see?	
4. What did he do?	
5. How long did it go on?	
6. How did he feel?	
7. What did he do next?	
8. What is his explanation?	
Headline:	

Part 1 Work in groups. Write three different sports in each category below. Explain the reason for your choices to your group.

scary	exciting	boring	interesting
_____	_____	_____	_____
_____	_____	_____	_____
_____	_____	_____	_____

Part 2 Have you ever done any of these sports? Talk about your experiences.

LISTEN TO THIS UNIT 12

Class CD 2
Track 68

Part 1 You are going to hear a panel discussion about censorship on the Internet. Listen to the discussion and check (✔) whether the speakers are *for* or *against*. Make notes about their main reasons.

	For	Against	Main reason
Roger			
Tomomi			
Antonio			
Frank			

Part 2 Can you add any more arguments for or against this topic? What is your opinion?

GIVE IT A TRY

Work in groups. Think of a famous book or movie. Describe the characters and the story and give your opinion about it. The rest of the group will guess the title. The person who guesses correctly gets one point.

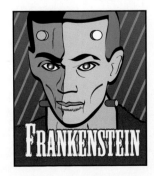

(Students C and D look at this page. Students A and B look at page 9.)

Part 1 Students C and D read the information below. Imagine that you and your partner meet at a party for new students. Make small talk and find out three interesting facts about your partner.

Student C: Andrew / Andrea Conlin
Your information:
You went to high school in Australia.
You practice yoga every day.
You recently went on vacation to India to study yoga.
You think that you met student D at a rock concert last month, but you don't remember his or her name.

Student D: Michael / Michelle Wu
Your information:
You were on the swim team in high school.
You love techno music and you are a DJ in your spare time.
You recently went to Guam to go scuba diving.
You think that you met Student C at a rock concert last month, but you don't remember his or her name.

Part 2 Now work with Students A and B. Everyone takes turns introducing his or her partner to the rest of the group. The rest of the group asks questions to continue the conversation.

Now Try This

Make new groups of four. Introduce your partner to the other two students. Add some information about your partner. It can be true or false. Your partner agrees or disagrees. Continue the conversation.

(Student B looks at this page. Student A looks at page 17.)

Part 1 Student A has recently moved to the town on the map below. Answer his or her questions about where to find some goods and services.

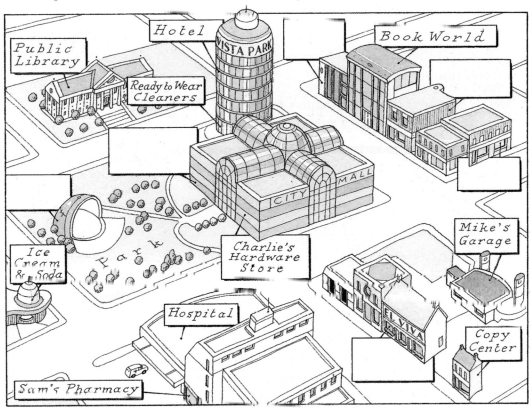

Part 2 You have moved to the town also. Ask questions to find out where you can do the following. Write the names of the places on the map above.

1. get your hair cut
2. listen to music
3. get your shoes repaired
4. go out for a meal
5. buy flowers
6. get your bicycle fixed

Now Try This

Choose two or three places in your neighborhood that provide goods and services. Tell your partner where they are and how to recognize where they are located.

(Student B looks at this page. Student A looks at page 25.)

Part 1 You are Pete Saito, a member of an unknown pop music group called Sound Bite. You are going to call Soundz Eazy recording studio.

1. Ask to speak with Ed Black, an executive at the studio.
2. Try to make an appointment to see him today.
3. If he isn't there, leave a message.
4. Your number is 591-555-6559.

Part 2 You are Chris, Pete Saito's roommate. Pete has gone out and you answer the phone for him. Take a message and get as much information as you can.

NOTES

Part 3 You are Pete Saito. After reading your roommate's message, call the studio again. Ask for information about getting an audition. Ask for additional information about renting the recording studio and sound equipment.

Now Try This

You are a receptionist at your school or college. Your partner is a new student calling for information. Role-play the conversation.

(Student B looks at this page. Student A looks at page 35.)

Part 1 You are a counselor for your partner. Listen carefully to his or her problem. Ask questions so that you understand the problem completely. Then give three suggestions about what your partner should do.

Your problem:

Your friend is going to start a new company on the Internet. You love designing websites and you want to join your friend in starting this new company. The problem is, you need to invest some money. Your friend says that you will double your investment in two years, but you don't have any money. You asked your parents, but they said it's too risky and you shouldn't waste your time. Also, the bank interest rates are too high. If you don't do this now, you'll never have another chance.

Suggestions:

1. _____

2. _____

3. _____

Part 2 Your partner is now a counselor. You are going to talk to him or her about the problem below. Read the description of the problem carefully and then explain it. Answer any questions your counselor asks. Listen carefully and write down his or her suggestions.

Part 3 Do you like the suggestions that your partner gave? Discuss with your partner why each one would or would not work.

Now Try This

Think of a real problem that you had in the past. How did you solve it? Tell your partner about the problem and see what advice he or she can suggest. Then compare the advice with what really happened.

(Student B looks at this page. Student A looks at page 51.)

Part 1 You suffer from insomnia (inability to sleep). For the past week, you have slept only two hours a night and you are exhausted. You have tried listening to relaxing music. It is not working because you are still falling asleep in class every afternoon. Listen to your partner's suggestions, choose the best one, and ask about any special instructions.

Write the suggestion here:

_____

Part 2 Student A suffers from migraines (strong and painful headaches). Think of a few different possible solutions to this problem and make a list. Then listen carefully to your partner's problem. Recommend the best remedies from your list.

Answer any questions about special instructions for using these remedies.

Part 3 Work in groups. Compare the suggestions each person chose in your group. How many people had the same suggestion?

Now Try This

Think of a common health problem that you or someone you know has had. Tell your partner about the problem and ask for advice.

(Student B looks at this page. Student A looks at page 69.)

Part 1 Read the hotel brochure. Answer your partner's questions about the hotel brochure.

CITY GARDEN HOTEL

*R*ELAX IN COMFORT AND STYLE!

Choose one of our 450 luxurious double-, queen-, or king-size guest rooms and 10 deluxe suites. The guest rooms feature individually controlled air conditioning and heating units, refrigerators, and _____.

Don't miss the opportunity of a wonderful dinner at Casa Rosa, a fusion of American, Asian, and _____ food. Open from 8 P.M. to midnight.

*S*ervices

Complimentary Internet access in our business center.

Fitness center passes available from the _____.

Cable TV available in deluxe suites only.

Wake-up calls from _____A.M. to noon.

Rooms equipped with:
Iron and ironing board /Hairdryer / Alarm / Radio

Garage parking ($27)

*R*ates

Single / Double room – $69

Queen-size room – $89

King-size room – $109

Deluxe suite – $_____

City tour – $35

City tour and dinner for two – $_____

Weekend Getaway Special (certain dates only) – $199

Room service available from our courteous concierge staff.
Newspaper delivered to guest rooms every weekday morning.
Limousine: Complimentary shuttle service to and from _____.
Fitness center: Indoor heated pool, sauna, whirlpool, massage, and weight room.

SPECIAL OFFERS:
Don't miss our special weekend getaway—two nights in a deluxe suite with _____ for two.

Part 2 Now, ask your partner questions about the hotel brochure to fill in the missing information.

Part 3 You are a desk clerk at this hotel. Your partner is a tourist. Answer his or her questions and write down the details of the reservation. Use the brochure above.

Now Try This

Describe your dream hotel. Tell your partner about it and answer his or her questions.

(Student B looks at this page. Student A looks at page 77.)

Part 1 You are a tourist visiting Vancouver for one day. You are staying at the Hotel Vancouver. Look at the map. What kinds of places are you interested in visiting? What places do you want more information about?

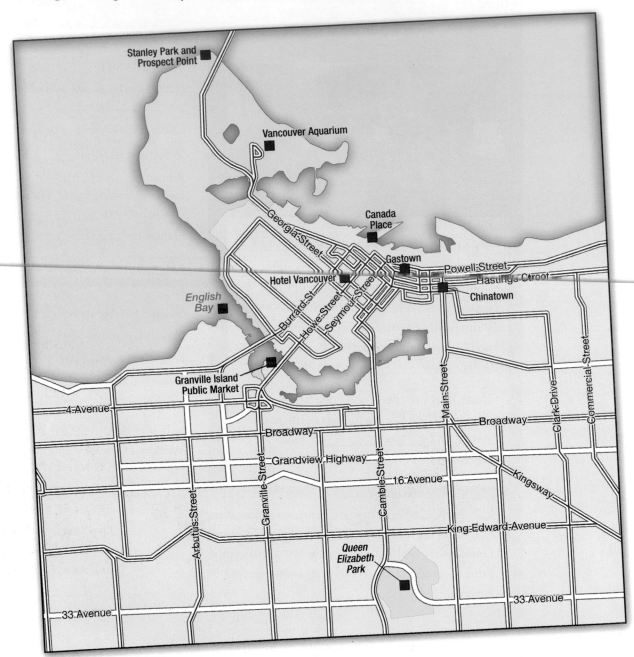

Part 2 Your partner is a tour guide. Ask your partner for advice on which sights you want to visit and ask how to get there from the Hotel Vancouver.

Part 3 You are only in Vancouver one day. What places will you definitely visit? Why? Compare your answers with your partner.

Now Try This

Choose another town or city that you know. Give your partner advice about what to see and do there.

(Student B looks at this page. Student A looks at page 87.)

Part 1 Read the following statements spoken by different people. What kind of person do you think said each statement? Write the adjective next to each one.

conceited	confident	outgoing	shy	argumentative
supportive	greedy	kind	rude	hardworking

When I am in class,...	Adjective
1. I don't mind speaking in front of the class.	
2. I encourage everyone to speak when we are working in a group.	
3. I often argue with the teacher.	
4. I usually wait for the teacher to ask me a question.	
5. I offer to help my partner when he or she needs it.	
6. I try to talk to all the students in the class.	
7. I usually think I know more than the other students.	
8. I want the teacher to pay the most attention to me.	
9. I always do all of my homework.	
10. If I disagree with someone, I tell them right away.	

Part 2 Your partner has different statements. Take turns reading the statements aloud and match the ones you think were said by the same people.

Part 3 Look at the list of jobs below. Your partner has a different list of jobs. Decide which person above is right for each job.

accountant

baker

writer

actor

pilot

Now Try This

Which statements in Part 1 are true for you? Tell your partner. Ask for advice about which job would be good for you.

(Student B looks at this page. Student A looks at page 103.)

Part 1 Read the survey on the topic of learning English. Write A if you agree, or D if you disagree.

Questionnaire
about Speaking Skills in English

		You	Your Partner
1	It is easier to speak English than to write it.		
2	The most difficult thing about speaking English is the pronunciation.		
3	It doesn't matter if I make mistakes when I am speaking English, as long as people understand me.		
4	To speak English well, I need a large vocabulary.		
5	If I am good at grammar, I will be able to speak English well.		
6	When I speak English, I usually translate from my native language in my mind.		
7	Reading, listening, and writing in English can help improve my speaking skills.		
8	Learning in a group helps me improve my speaking skills.		

What advice would you give to someone just starting to learn English on how to improve their speaking skills?

Part 2 Student A will interview you about learning English. Give reasons for your opinions. Reverse roles. Interview Student A. Ask for reasons for his or her opinions. Make notes about your partner's reasons. Agree or disagree and respond with your own reasons.

Part 3 Use the notes about your partner's reasons to report to the class on your interview. Summarize your partner's opinions.

Now Try This

Work in pairs. Choose another topic in your school and make up a survey. Exchange surveys with another pair and interview them. Then report to the class.

Audio script

Unit 1

GIVE IT A TRY   **PAGE 3**

1. Conversational openings
A: This is a great film festival, isn't it?
B: It sure is. This film looks wonderful.
A: It sure does.

2. Extending the conversation
A: This is a great film festival, isn't it?
B: It sure is. The films are wonderful.
A: Have you been to this film festival before?
B: Yes, I was here last year.

3. Asking if you've met before
A: Don't I know you from somewhere?
B: I'm not sure. Do you?
A: I think we met at Sam's birthday party.
B: Oh, yes. I remember you now.
A: My name's Pete. Pete Wilson.
B: I'm Liz Wu.

LISTEN TO THIS   **PAGE 4**

1
M: There are a lot of people in this class, aren't there?
L: Yes, I didn't know it would be so crowded.
M: Do you mind if I share your book just for today's class? I haven't bought mine yet.
L: Sure. No problem. Haven't we met somewhere before?
M: I'm not sure…. Were you in Mrs. Brown's English class last semester?
L: No, I wasn't. I took French last semester. Maybe we met at registration or something.
M: Yes! That was it! You were next to me in the line for registration last week.
L: Nice to see you again! My name's Lee.
M: I'm Mike.

2
R: This food looks really delicious!
E: Yes, it does. The bride looks so happy, too.
R: Are you a friend of Janet's?
E: Yes, I am. We went to high school together. How about you?
R: I'm a friend of hers too, from college. But I have the feeling we've met before somewhere….
E: Have we? Were you at Janet's twenty-first birthday party?
R: Yes, I was! I remember now, you were sitting at the other end of the table.
E: Yes, nice to meet you finally! I'm Eve.
R: Nice to meet you, too. My name's Ruth.

3
S: There are so many people here, but no one that I really recognize. Have you seen anyone you know yet? Wait a minute…. Aren't you Joe Simpson?
J: Yes, I am.
S: I'm Stan MacDonald. We were on the soccer team together, remember?
J: Yes, that's right! Good to see you again, Stan.
S: It's good to see you, too. You haven't changed a bit!
J: I don't play much now, though. Did you see that match between England and Brazil?

GIVE IT A TRY   **PAGE 7**

1. Introducing friends
A: Luis, this is my friend Eun-joo. Eun-joo, this is Luis. We met in class last year.
B: Hi, Luis. It's nice to meet you.
C: Hello, Eun-joo. It's nice to meet you, too.

2. Making small talk (1)
A: I hear you're a good bass player.
B: I'm not bad. Do you play music?
A: Yes, I do. I play keyboards.
B: How often do you play?
A: Every weekend.

3. Making small talk (2)
A: Luis, this is my friend Eun-joo.
B: Hi, Luis, it's nice to meet you.
C: It's nice to meet you, too.
A: Luis just got back from Hong Kong.
B: Really? How was it?
C: It was amazing.

LISTEN TO THIS   **PAGE 8**

1
S: Hi, Marta! Are you going to the movies with us after class tonight?
M: Hi, Steve! Sure. I'd love to. By the way, have you met my cousin Tammy? She's visiting us from New York for a few days.
S: Hi, Tammy. Nice to meet you.
T: Nice to meet you, too.
M: Tammy's just seen the latest Johnny Depp movie.
S: Really? How was it?
T: Awesome. I love Johnny Depp.

2
J: Excuse me. Sorry to disturb you. I'd like to introduce Oliver Johnson. He's our marketing consultant in Brazil. He's visiting our offices for a couple of days.
S: How do you do, Oliver? I'm pleased to meet you. My name's Sam Perez, and I'm the chief financial officer.
O: I am very glad to meet you.
J: Oliver has just returned from a trip to Japan to research marketing strategies over there.
S: Was it interesting?
O: Yes, fascinating!
S: I want to hear all about it. Julie, let's all have coffee together later on so we can talk more.
J: Great idea.
S: See you both later then. Oliver, please enjoy your visit to our offices.
O: Thank you.

3
J: Hi, Max! I haven't seen you in a while!
M: Oh, hi…Janice.
T: (to Janice) I don't think we've met, have we?
M: Oh, uh…Tina, this is Janice, a…friend of mine from high school.
T: Hi, Janice, I'm Tina, Max's girlfriend. Nice to meet you.
J: Max and I are very old friends! How long have you known each other?
T: Not that long. We met on a skiing trip in the Alps last winter.
J: A skiing trip? How romantic! You must be a good skier.
T: I'm not bad. Do you ski?
J: No, I prefer snowboarding.

Unit 2

GIVE IT A TRY   **PAGE 11**

1. Asking where services are located
PRACTICE 1
A: Excuse me. Where can I get my shirt cleaned?
B: I think there's a dry cleaner's in the mall across the street.

PRACTICE 2
A: Excuse me. Do you know where I can buy a new shirt?
B: You can try the store on Washington Street. It's next to the King Building.

2. Describing buildings
A: Which one is the King Building?
B: It's the big glass office building just past the park.

LISTEN TO THIS   **PAGE 12**

B: Hi, Kumiko. Hey! What's the matter?
K: It's my boyfriend's birthday tomorrow, and I have no idea what to get him.
B: No ideas at all?
K: Well, he needs a new baseball glove. I just went to the Athletic Center, but I couldn't afford the one he really wants. Everything there is way too expensive.

B: Did you try Sports World?

K: I've never heard of it.

B: It's a brand new store, so they're having all sorts of opening week specials. Almost everything is 30 or 40 percent off.

K: Great. Where is it?

B: On Duncan Street.

K: Where is it on Duncan?

B: Do you know the Manning Building?

K: Is that the big yellow office building beside the Metro Hotel?

B: No, that's the Manulife Building. The Manning Building is the tall, glass building across from the hospital. It has a restaurant and observation deck at the top.

K: OK. I know where it is then.

B: Sports World is right beside that.

K: I'll go over there right after lunch. Thanks!

B: Glad to help. Good luck!

1. Asking for directions in a store (1)

A: Could you tell me where I can find an umbrella?

B: In the accessories department, on the second floor.

2. Asking for directions in a store (2)

A: I'm looking for an umbrella. Where can I find them, please?

B: Umbrellas are on this floor. Walk down here to your left. They're across from the perfume counter.

3. Asking for directions in a mall

A: I need to buy a new shirt. Where can I find a women's clothing store?

B: There is a women's clothing store on this level.

1

M: Excuse me. Does your store sell running shoes? I was in the shoe department but I didn't see any running shoes…or sales clerks.

C: I'm sorry about that. Our running shoes are in Sporting Goods.

M: That makes sense. And where is that department?

C: Sporting Goods is on two. The second floor.

M: Thank you.

2

W: Excuse me. Where's your furniture department?

C: It's on the sixth floor.

W: Do they sell tables and chairs for outside?

C: No. All our outdoor furniture is in the Garden Shop. But that's also on six. Just be sure to turn left when you get off the escalator.

W: I will. Thanks very much.

3

C: Can I help you?

M: Yes, please. I bought this stereo here last week, and it's not working properly. Where is your repair department?

C: Take that to the electronics department, where you bought it. They'll take care of it for you.

M: Back to the electronics department? OK. That's on the third floor isn't it?

C: Yes, that's right.

Unit 3

1. Asking to speak to someone

PRACTICE 1

A: Hello.

B: Hi. Could I please speak to Jo?

A: Speaking.

PRACTICE 2

A: Hello.

B: Hi. Is Jo there, please?

A: Sure, just a moment, please. I'll get her.

2. Offering to take a message

A: Hello.

B: Hi, could I please speak to John?

A: I'm sorry he's not here right now. Could I take a message?

B: No, thanks. I'll call back later.

3. Taking a Message

A: Hello?

B: Hi. Could I please speak to John?

A: Sorry, he's not here right now. Can I take a message?

B: Yes, please.

A: Just a moment. Let me get a pen…. All right, go ahead.

B: This is Hong-an Li, and my number is 312-364-0107. Could you ask John to call me?

A: Sure. I'll give him the message as soon as he gets in.

1

Mrs. W: Hello?

P: Hello. Is Ted there, please?

Mrs. W: I'm sorry. He isn't home right now. Could I take a message?

P: This is Pete Anderson. I'm calling about the school chess competition next weekend. Could you ask him to give me a call?

Mrs. W: Sure. Does Ted have your number?

P: I'll give it to you just in case. It's 671-599-7671.

Mrs. W: OK. 671-599-7671. Pete Anderson. About the chess competition.

P: That's it. Thank you.

Mrs. W: You're welcome. Bye now.

2

Mrs. S: Hello?

E: Hi, Mrs. Samuels. This is Emma. Can I speak to Debbie, please?

Mrs. S: She's not in right now. Can I take a message?

E: Yes, please. Can you tell her the time of the test tomorrow has changed from 10:30 to 9:30? Mrs. Wilson phoned to tell me there was a mistake in the schedule.

Mrs. S: Oh, my goodness! That is important. Of course I'll tell her as soon as she gets in.

E: Thanks a lot.

Mrs. S: You're welcome. Good-bye, dear.

E: Good-bye.

1. Calling for information

A: Good morning. Admissions Office. Can I help you?

B: Yes, please. I am interested in taking a language class. Could you tell me how to apply?

A: Yes, of course. You just need to fill out an application form and send it to us with the registration fee.

B: Great. Could you send me a form, please? My name is Hong-an Li, H-o-n-g (dash) a-n, L-i, and my address is 4211 South Main Street, Chicago, 60614.

A: OK, we'll send that out to you right away.

2. Asking for additional information

A: I'd also like some information about student housing, please.

B: Sure, you can speak to our student housing coordinator. Hold on, please. I'll see if she is available.

3. Leaving a message

A: I'm sorry the housing coordinator's line is busy right now. Could I have your number?

B: Yes, of course. My number is 312-364-0107.

A: I'll see she gets back to you very soon.

B: Thank you.

1

A: Good afternoon. University of Miami.

B: Yes. Good afternoon. I'd like to speak to the Student Housing Office, please.

A: Hold the line. I'll connect you. I'm sorry. All the lines are busy right now. Could you call back later?

B: Sure. Thank you.

2

A: Good afternoon. Medical Clinic.

B: Is Dr. Adams available, please?

A: I'm sorry. He's on vacation this week. Can another doctor help you?

B: No, I don't think so. When will Dr. Adams be back in the office?

A: He'll be back on Monday morning.

B: OK. I'll call back then.

3

A: Computer City. How can I help you?

B: I'd like to speak to the technical support department, please.

A: Is there anyone in particular you want to speak to?

B: No. Just technical support. I only have one quick question.

A: OK. I'll put you through.

4

A: Global Travel. Good morning.

B: Good morning. Is Nancy Green there, please?

A: Yes, she's here, but she's with a customer right now. Can I take a message and have her call you back?

B: All right. My name is Peggy O'Hara, and my number is 361-444-1416.

Review Unit 1

LISTEN TO THIS   PAGE 26

T: I hope this class won't be too difficult. I'm not good at math.

S: Neither am I. You know, I think we've met somewhere before, haven't we?

T: I'm not sure. Have we?

S: Weren't you in that history class last semester with Mr. Smith?

T: Yeah, I was.

S: Yes, you sat in the front row. I was two rows behind. You probably didn't see me. Anyway, my name's Sophie. Nice to meet you.

T: Nice to meet you, too. I'm Tran.

S: Do you want to go for a coffee after class today?

T: That would be nice.

Review Unit 2

LISTEN TO THIS   PAGE 26

1

Turn right at the next corner. Keep walking past the food court, turn right again, it's next to the coffee shop.

2

Turn right at the bookstore, keep going until you see the toy store, it's about three stores down, on your right.

3

It's across from the juice bar, between the jeans and the sports clothing store. You can't miss it.

Review Unit 3

LISTEN TO THIS   PAGE 27

1

V: Hi. You have reached the Johnson's. We can't come to the phone right now, but if

you leave your name, number, and a brief message, we'll get back to you as soon as we can.

D: This is a message for Mrs. Johnson. This is Debbie. I can't baby-sit on Friday night, but a friend of mine can if you want. She has lots of experience baby-sitting. Her name is Mary Ann, and her phone number is, uh, 209-892-2971. Bye.

2

V: Hi. This is Dave Summers. I can't talk right now, but leave your name, number, and a brief message and I'll call you back.

R: Hi, Dave, this is Ron. Something's come up and I can't make it to the show tomorrow night. You're going to be mad at me, I know, but listen, Barry says he can play the bass for some of our tunes. He's heard us playing them enough times! Give him a try. His number is 677-439-2121.

3

V: Hi. This is Michiko Saito. I can't come to the phone right now, but if you leave your name, number, and a message, I'll call you back as soon as I can.

T: Hi, Michi. This is Tammy. Want to come to a party on Friday night? Call me if you can, 607-690-2541.

Unit 4

GIVE IT A TRY   PAGE 29

1. Identifying a problem

A: It's really a problem when people bring their cell phones to class.

B: I know what you mean. It's not polite and it disturbs everyone.

2. Making suggestions

A: What can we do about students using cell phones in class?

B: We can have a sign on the wall that says, "Remember to turn off your cell phones."

A: That's a good idea.

C: Let's have a fine for anyone whose cell phone rings in class.

B: That's too complicated.

LISTEN TO THIS   PAGE 30

Good evening, ladies and gentlemen, and welcome. I'm sure we have all heard the expression, "Think Green." Tonight we are going to talk about ways that we can "Act Green" in our everyday lives.

The best place to start, of course, is in the home. Every day, people all over the world are hurting the environment without even knowing it. For example, busy families buy paper napkins and towels at the supermarket. This helps them save time on housework, but after these things have been used, what happens to them? They go in the trash. In many places, especially in North America, big cities are running out of places to throw

their trash. What can we do about this? How can we cut down on garbage?

Well, we can start using cloth napkins and cloth towels instead of paper towels. When we go grocery shopping, we can choose products that are not overpackaged. For example, last week I bought a package of cookies. The cookies were in a bag, there was a plastic tray inside the bag, and then each cookie was in its own little package on the tray in the bag! That's overpackaging! We should also take our own bags to the grocery store to carry things home in.

Cleaning products are another danger. Dangerous cleaning products enter our water supply every day. Of course, everyone wants a clean house—so what's the answer? For one thing, we could make our own cleaning products from natural ingredients like baking soda, lemon, and vinegar.

Now, how about in the community? At work and school, we use one very valuable item every day. Paper. Of course, we need paper to do our work, but how much do we waste? Get your school or office to recycle paper. Learn to make notepads from the unused sides of old pieces of paper. Finally, plant a tree. Better yet, plant two trees!

GIVE IT A TRY   PAGE 33

1. Asking for and giving advice

A: What's the problem?

B: Ken is the cheapest guy I've ever gone out with. What should I do?

A: You should start looking for a new boyfriend!

2. Describing consequences

A: What's the problem?

B: Ken is the cheapest guy I've ever gone out with. What should I do?

A: Why don't you talk to him about it?

B: If I criticize him, he'll get mad at me!

A: In that case, I think you should start looking for a new boyfriend!

LISTEN TO THIS   PAGE 34

1

F: Hi, Luisa.

L: Hi.

F: What's the matter?

L: I have a problem with my mom.

F: Do you want to talk about it?

L: Well…my mother said I can't go to David's birthday party on Thursday night.

F: How come?

L: Because it's a school night and I have some big tests next week. She wants me to stay home and study. I really want to go. I don't know what to do.

F: Why don't you promise to come home early?

2

J: …and then we'll go for coffee. Is that OK with you, Elaine? Elaine? Are you listening?

E: What? Oh, sorry. What did you say?

J: What's the problem, Elaine? Are you worried about something?

E: It's my boyfriend. He wants to go and live in Australia.

J: Does he have a job over there or something?

E: Yes, he does and he wants me to go, too.

J: Do you want to go?

E: That's the problem. I'm not sure if I want to or not.

J: Well, maybe you should talk it over with your family. That might help you to decide.

3

M: That Brendan is driving me crazy!

T: Why? What's the matter?

M: He's always borrowing little things, and he never returns them.

T: Like what?

M: Oh, you know, pencils, paper, money for a coffee, bus tickets—I'm starting to feel like his mother! What would you do?

T: Well, I'd tell him you're sorry, but you just can't keep on giving stuff to him any more.

M: I guess you're right.

Unit 5

1. Asking about other people

A: Have you heard about Eun-mi?

B: No, I haven't. How's she doing these days?

A: So-so.

2. Reacting to good and bad news

A: Have you heard about Eun-mi?

B: How's she doing these days?

A: So-so. She broke her arm.

B: That's terrible.

3. Asking for more details

A: How's Eun-mi doing these days?

B: So-so. She broke her arm.

A: That's terrible. How did it happen?

B: Well, she went skiing during winter vacation….

1

S: Have you heard what happened to Ellen's parents?

P: No, what happened?

S: The roof of their house was blown off by a tornado.

P: That's awful! Are they OK? Where are they going to live?

S: They're fine. They're staying with Ellen's brother right now. What's really bad is that the house wasn't covered by insurance.

P: Oh, that's really bad news.

2

J: Have you heard about Steve?

S: No, what happened to him?

J: Well, he applied for a job as a script assistant at a big movie company. He had to take some sort of test.

S: A test? What kind of test?

J: Oh, I don't know, some kind of grammar or spelling test, I suppose. Anyway, he failed the test, but they gave him a job as a movie extra instead. Isn't that great?

S: Good for him! So he'll be in the movies now?

J: Yeah, he's really ecstatic.

3

N: What's going on with Dan these days? I haven't seen him for a while.

G: Well, he hasn't been too good recently. You know he lost his job, don't you?

N: Oh, no! Why? What happened?

G: His company went bankrupt. They didn't even pay him his last month's salary.

N: That's too bad. What's he going to do now?

G: He couldn't decide what to do at first, but I think he's going to move to California and look for a job out there.

N: I hope it works out.

1. Saying what someone should have done

A: Did you hear about Brenda?

B: No, what happened?

A: Brenda caught Stan kissing another woman.

B: She should have left him right away!

2. Asking for details

A: Did you hear about Brenda?

B: No, what happened?

A: She was driving too fast and had an accident.

B: Was she hurt?

A: She broke her arm.

3. Interrupting and getting back to the story

A: Did you hear about Brenda? She ended up at the hospital. She was…

B: Wait a minute. Why did she go to the hospital?

A: She was driving too fast and had an accident. Anyway…

B: Was she hurt?

A: She broke her arm. But listen, the important thing is that she fell in love with the doctor who fixed her arm.

B: Let me get this straight. Brenda caught Stan with another woman, got into a car accident, and now she's going out with her doctor? That's unbelievable.

J: Did you hear about what happened to Dave and Meg when they went climbing in the Alps last year?

S: No, what happened?

J: They were caught in a sudden snowstorm and got trapped on a narrow ledge. Dave hurt his foot and couldn't climb.

S: That's terrible! What did they do?

J: They put up their tent to try and keep warm and have shelter from the snow.

S: Did they have any food with them?

J: They just had one chocolate bar.

S: One chocolate bar? Why didn't they have more food?

J: Well, they were on their way down and they had eaten almost all of their supplies. Anyway, luckily Meg had her cell phone with her. The signal was very weak, but she managed to call her friend in Geneva and….

S: In Geneva! Why didn't she phone the emergency services?

J: Because the signal was too weak, and the batteries were almost dead. But listen, the main thing is, her friend was able to get through to the mountain rescue team, and they sent a helicopter to rescue them.

S: How long were they trapped there?

J: Oh, about 16 hours.

S: That's incredible. They could have frozen to death!

Unit 6

1. Talking about symptoms

A: You look a little feverish. Are you OK?

B: To tell you the truth, I feel terrible.

A: Why? What's the matter?

B: I have a horrible headache and a sore throat.

2. Giving, accepting, and refusing advice

A: What's the matter?

B: I have a horrible headache.

A: You'd better take some aspirin.

B: That's a good idea. I'll give it a try.

3. Advising someone *not* to do something

A: You look terrible. What's the matter?

B: I have a horrible headache and a sore throat.

A: Maybe you shouldn't go to class today.

B: But I have a test this afternoon!

T: Jake? Are you OK? You look a little pale.

J: Yeah, I didn't sleep well last night. I had this terrible pain in my knee. I think I strained it when I went cycling yesterday.

T: Maybe you shouldn't go out today. Why don't you take some aspirin and lie down?

J: Aspirin makes my stomach feel funny. Do we still have any of the pain relieving gel that I used for my backache?

T: I'm not sure. I'll take a look. Or why don't you use the heating pad? That really worked well on my back last time.

J: I suppose so. You used an ice pack, too, didn't you?

T: Yes, but that didn't really work.

J: OK. I'll try the heating pad first and then I'll put on some of that gel…if we have any left.

GIVE IT A TRY — PAGE 49

1. Asking for advice

A: What do you think I should take for a headache?

B: You could try this pain reliever.

2. Giving instructions

A: I have a terrible headache and a fever. What do you think I should take?

B: You could try this fever reducer.

A: How often do I have to take it?

B: Take two tablets every six hours with food. Your fever should come down within 24 hours.

3. Asking about instructions

A: Are there any special instructions?

B: You must take these with food.

A: Am I allowed to take aspirin with this medication?

B: No, you shouldn't take any aspirin.

LISTEN TO THIS — PAGE 50

1

P: Good morning. What can I do for you?

C: Oh, this is embarrassing….

P: Don't worry. How can I help?

C: I'm looking for something for pimples. What do you recommend?

P: This cream is very good. Use it every morning and evening after washing your face.

C: Should I use a lot or just a little?

P: Just a little, otherwise your skin will dry out.

C: OK. I'll take it. Thanks.

2

C: Excuse me. Can you help me?

P: Certainly.

C: I wonder if you have anything for backaches.

P: This ointment is very good.

C: I've used that. It didn't really help. The thing is, I sit at the computer about ten hours a day. I think that's the problem.

P: One of these might help.

C: What is it?

P: It's a back-support cushion.

C: Are there any special instructions?

P: Try not to lean forward when you work. Sit with your back straight so that your knees, hips, and elbows form right angles. And take frequent breaks to stretch your muscles.

C: OK. I'll give it a try. Thanks a lot.

3

P: Is there something I can help you with, ma'am?

C: Yes, please! I really need something for this sunburn.

P: Too much sun is dangerous, you know.

C: I know, but I fell asleep at the beach.

P: Try this sunburn lotion. It'll help the pain. It's also got a moisturizer in it.

C: How often do I put this on?

P: Every two hours, until the pain subsides.

C: Is there anything else I can do?

P: Well, you could try soaking in a cool bath for 20 minutes before putting the lotion on your skin.

C: Thanks a lot.

Review Unit 4

LISTEN TO THIS — PAGE 52

Today I'm going to talk to you about the problem of increasing traffic in our cities. First, I will describe some of the effects caused by too many cars in our cities. Then I will suggest a few possible solutions.

What are some of the effects caused by too many cars in our cities?

First, cars use a lot of space. Think of all the space needed for parking and driving, and think what a difference it would make if it were used instead for parks, trees, and recreation areas.

Second, cars create a lot of air and noise pollution. Our cities are getting dirtier and noisier and more unhealthy every day. Just think how much healthier we would be if there were fewer cars.

Third, cars are dangerous. Cars cause hundreds of accidents, injuries, and deaths in our cities every year.

Well, you are going to ask, what can we do about it? We can't forbid people to buy or use their cars, can we?

There are a number of solutions available that have been tried in various cities around the world.

One is to create pedestrian or car-free zones. At least there will be some areas of the city where people can walk in peace and safety.

Another solution is to charge private cars for entering the city and increase parking fees. If it becomes cheaper to use public transportation, people will avoid using their cars unless it is really necessary.

A third way is to encourage people to use public transportation by improving public transportation services, offering special discounts and reasonable prices so that buses and trains are cheaper and more convenient.

Now, if you have any questions….

Review Unit 5

LISTEN TO THIS — PAGE 52

1

W: Did I tell you about Dave and Atsuko?

M: No. What?

W: They're going to get married!

M: That's great news!

W: You know Dave's been asking her to marry him for quite a long time and she finally said yes!

M: So when's the wedding?

W: Next month.

2

W: How's Debbie doing these days?

M: Oh, didn't you hear about her new job? She's going to teach English in Italy.

W: Oh, that's fantastic! When will she be leaving?

M: In August.

W: I bet she's really excited about that.

3

M: Have you heard about what happened to Marco on vacation?

W: No, what happened?

M: He was on vacation in Australia, when someone broke into his hotel room and stole all his money and his passport.

W: That's terrible! What did he do?

M: Fortunately, he had a photocopy of his passport, which he kept separately. He took that to the embassy and they managed to get him another passport within a few days.

W: That was lucky!

Review Unit 6

LISTEN TO THIS — PAGE 53

T: What's the matter, Shami? You're not walking too well.

S: Oh, Tom. I have this terrible pain in my knee.

T: I'm sorry to hear that.

S: My knee has swollen up and it's really bad when I go up and down the stairs like this.

T: Have you been to the doctor?

S: Yes, she said I should rest and she gave me some painkillers.

T: Have you tried anything else?

S: Well, my friend lent me a heating pad, and I tried that for a while, but it had no effect at all.

T: What about ice packs?

S: No. I haven't tried that yet. That's a good idea.

T: Also, there's a really good cream you can get from the pharmacy. When you rub it on your muscles, it makes the joints feel warm and it relieves some of the pain, too.

S: That sounds good. What's the name of it? I'll go and get some right away.

T: Hang on a minute. I'll write down the name for you.

Unit 7

GIVE IT A TRY — PAGE 55

1. Describing what objects are used for

A: What's this thing used for?

B: It's used for making ice cream.

2. Giving instructions

A: What's this thing?
B: It's an ice-cream maker.
A: How do you use it?
B: First, you put this metal container in the bottom of the tub….

LISTEN TO THIS   **PAGE 56**

Here's a quick and easy recipe for potato pancakes. Delicious as an appetizer or as a main course!

First, the ingredients. You'll need six medium potatoes, two eggs, two tablespoons of flour, one small onion, some vegetable oil, and a pinch of salt and pepper.

Now here's how to make them. First, grate the potatoes and squeeze them dry. Next, chop the onion. After that, mix together the eggs, flour, salt, and pepper. Then mix in the potatoes and the onion.

Finally, heat the oil in a frying pan, drop the potato mixture into the pan in small spoonfuls, and cook for three minutes on each side until they are brown and crisp.

Serve with applesauce and sour cream. That's it! Easy!

GIVE IT A TRY   **PAGE 59**

1. Discussing needs and requirements

A: Would you like to go to the beach for a barbie with us next weekend?
B: I'd love to come. Do I need to bring anything?
A: Yes, you need a hat.
B: What else do I need?
A: That's it.

2. Asking for clarification

A: What do I need insect repellent for?
B: It's to keep mosquitoes and other insects away.

3. Talking about consequences

A: Do I need to bring anything?
B: Yes, you need a hat.
A: Why do I need a hat?
B: If you don't wear a hat, you'll get sunburned.

LISTEN TO THIS   **PAGE 60**

H: Hi, Nicki! So, are you ready for my visit?
N: Yup! How about you? Are you ready to visit me?
H: I've got my skis, ski poles, and boots for skiing. What else?
N: You should have a pair of strong sunglasses to protect your eyes. The snow gets awfully bright. Did you pack any shorts?
H: Shorts! What do I need shorts for? I'm going there to ski.
N: I know. I thought you might want to wear them on really warm sunny days. And how could I forget? Sunscreen!
H: I know…for the sun, right?
N: Right. But really, bring some so you don't get a sunburn. Are you bringing a nice dress or anything?
H: Do I need one?

N: Bring one—but not too fancy—in case we all go out for a nice dinner one night.
H: OK. What else?
N: Bring lots of comfortable clothes for relaxing in.
H: Great idea. I'm looking forward to sitting around in front of the fire after a day of skiing.

Unit 8

GIVE IT A TRY   **PAGE 63**

1. Asking about types of hotels

A: We'd like to book a hotel in Tioman, please.
B: Are you interested in a hotel or a package?
A: Well, a package would be better.
B: Take a look at this brochure.
A: This looks perfect.

2. Asking for details

A: Where is the Spa Resort Hotel?
B: It's on the beach
A: Does it have a swimming pool?
B: Yes, it does.

3. Making a reservation

A: I'd like to reserve a double room at the Spa Resort Hotel, please.
B: Certainly. For what dates?
A: From September 23–30.
B: Could I have your name, please?
A: Yes, my last name is Park. P-a-r-k.

LISTEN TO THIS   **PAGE 64**

C: Palm Tree Hotel. How can I help you?
Ms. G: Oh, hello. Could you tell me if you have any rooms free for Thursday and Friday next week?
C: For how many people?
Ms. G: A single room, please.
C: Yes, we have a single room available, that's no problem.
Ms. G: OK, I'd like to make a reservation, please. The name is Gardiner. G-a-r-d-i-n-e-r. Ms. Emily Gardiner. And it's for two nights from June 28–30.
C: OK, check in any time after 3:00 P.M. and your room will be ready.
Ms. G: Oh, could you make sure it is a non-smoking room, please? I just can't stand the smell of cigarette smoke.
C: Yes, certainly.
Ms. G: And could you make sure it is a quiet room? I don't want to be overlooking the parking lot or anything like that.
C: Yes, of course.
Ms. G: Does the room price include breakfast?
C: Yes, it does. Breakfast is served in our restaurant from 7:00 A.M.
Ms. G: That's good. I'd like to not be too far away from the restaurant, please. Do all the rooms have cable TV?

C: Yes, they do.
Ms. G: And room service?
C: Yes, you'll find a flyer containing all the information about our hotel services in your room. If you have any questions, just call the front desk.
Ms. G: OK. Thank you. Oh, just one more thing.
C: Yes?
Ms. G: How much does it cost?

GIVE IT A TRY   **PAGE 67**

1. Checking in

A: I'd like to check in, please.
B: Do you have a reservation?
A: Yes, the last name is Park.
B: Here it is. Could you sign here, please?

2. Making requests

A: Do you have a room with an ocean view?
B: Yes, certainly. You can have room 43B.

3. Asking about hotel services

A: Can I help you?
B: Could you tell me what time the restaurant opens for breakfast?
A: Yes, of course. Breakfast is served in the restaurant from 7:30 A.M. to 10:00 A.M.
B: Thank you very much.

LISTEN TO THIS   **PAGE 68**

1

Mr. M: I'd like to check in, please.
C: Certainly. Do you have a reservation?
Mr. M: Yes. The name is Morales. Mr. and Mrs. J. Morales.
C: Here we are. For five nights. Could you fill out the registration card, please? And I'll need your credit card.
Mr. M: All right.
C: Thank you. And here's your room key. Room 826.
Mr. M: Does that room have an ocean view?
C: No. Rooms with an ocean view are $15.00 more per night. Your room overlooks…the parking lot.
Mr. M: Well, we'd like a room with an ocean view, please.
C: I'm sorry. Those rooms are all taken.

2

C: Front desk. Can I help you?
Mr. B: This is Mr. Burton in 1205. Can I get a wake-up call, please?
C: Of course. What time?
Mr. B: Five o'clock.
C: That's no problem. We'll be happy to do that. Anything else?
Mr. B: No. That's it. Thank you.

3

G: (To herself) I really overslept. Oh, boy. Eleven o'clock. I need something to eat. I'm starving.
C: Front desk. Can I help you?
G: Yeah, hi. This is Gale Martin in room 327. Is breakfast still being served?
C: I'm sorry. Breakfast finishes at 10:30 A.M.

G: Oh, no. Well, do you know where I can get some breakfast?

C: Just call Room Service at extension 121. You can order some food from them. They'll send it up to your room.

G: OK, thanks. I'll give them a call.

Unit 9

GIVE IT A TRY   PAGE 71

1. Getting information

A: I need some ideas for things to do in Hong Kong.

B: What are you interested in seeing?

A: First, I want to see the famous sights.

B: You shouldn't miss Victoria Peak. You can get fantastic views from there. Then you can go shopping.

2. Discussing possible activities

A: What is there to do?

B: If you like shopping, there are lots of street markets.

A: I'm not really interested in that. What else is there to do?

LISTEN TO THIS   PAGE 72

1

Vietnam is the ideal holiday destination for travelers who like the unusual and the unique. Go sight-seeing in Hanoi, the 1,000-year-old capital city of Vietnam, a unique blend of eastern and western charm with brightly painted temples and pagodas side by side with elegant French colonial buildings.

Visit the Temple of Literature, the site of Vietnam's first university, which dates back to 1070, the One Pillar Pagoda, first built in 1049, which resembles a lotus blossom rising out of the water, and Ho Chi Minh's Mausoleum, the burial place of the famous leader who led Vietnam to independence.

Enjoy Hanoi's cuisine and linger over a cup of coffee in one of its sidewalk cafes. Spend an evening at the traditional water puppet theater. Originally performed on lakes and ponds, these productions take place in a theater with a stage knee-deep in water.

If you like shopping, you won't be bored! Browse the 36 streets of the Old Quarter where each street was originally named after the product sold there, for example, Fish Street, Tin Street, and Bamboo Street. Bargains include silk, embroidery, handicrafts, and original works of art.

2

Guam is a tropical paradise! The island's dramatic coastline and white sand beaches are ringed by coral reefs and crystal clear waters full of exotic marine life.

Visit the underwater observatories and discover 300 types of coral. Go diving for buried treasure among the shipwrecks. Take a boat tour to go dolphin-watching.

If you like water sports, the island of Guam is the place for you! There are ocean sports for the whole family, including banana boat rides, kayaking, pedal boats, parasailing, snorkeling, windsurfing, and wake boarding.

GIVE IT A TRY   PAGE 75

1. Asking about public transportation

A: Excuse me. What's the best way to get to Waterfront Park from here? Can I take a bus?

B: Yes, you can catch the number 34 bus.

2. Talking about tours

A: What does the city tour include?

B: They take you around the major points of interest.

LISTEN TO THIS   PAGE 76

G: Welcome aboard our trolleybus tour of downtown Minneapolis. We are delighted to have you aboard.

I'll be collecting your tickets in a moment. If you don't have your ticket yet, please go to the ticket stand on the corner, and they'll be happy to help you. Tickets are $20.00 each.

The tour lasts two hours. Our tour today includes all the highlights of our beautiful downtown and also the historic St. Anthony's Falls heritage zone. There will be a 30-minute break for lunch at the Nicollet Mall. That's a great place to stroll around, and the food court has a wide variety of meals and snacks. At the end of the tour, we'll drop you off right here where we picked you up, outside the Walker Art Center.

OK. My name is Annalisa and I'm going to be your guide today. I was born and brought up right here in Minneapolis, and I reckon I know the city pretty well. But you may well come up with a question I can't answer. That happens sometimes! Please ask questions. That makes the ride so much more interesting! And please tell me if you want to stop to take pictures. I'm happy to do that. Now where are you all from?

P: Florida! Japan! England!

Review Unit 7

LISTEN TO THIS   PAGE 78

First, let's talk about the things you'll need. You'll need some liquid glue, some newspaper torn into long strips, a balloon, some plastic food wrap, and a pin. OK? Got that?

Now let's talk about the instructions. The first thing you have to do is blow up the balloon. Next, cover the balloon with plastic food wrap. After that, cover the food wrap with glue. This gets really messy! OK, next take the strips of newspaper, and put them over the glued area. They should go around the balloon. Then cover it with glue again. You'll probably want to put 15 to 20 layers of newspaper on. After that, let it dry thoroughly. It might take a day or two. Finally, put a pin through it and pop the balloon, and there you have it!

Review Unit 8

LISTEN TO THIS   PAGE 78

C: Hi. Can I help you?

W: Yes, I'd like a room for the night, please. The sign outside says you have vacancies.

C: Yes, but only a couple.

W: How much are the rooms?

C: They're $50.00 a night.

W: That's fine.

C: I can give you room 14. I just need you to sign the register.

W: There you go. I'm awfully hungry. Is the restaurant still open?

C: We don't have a restaurant, but the coffee shop is open until nine o'clock. If you want anything after that, there are a couple of vending machines for soft drinks, chocolate bars—things like that.

W: Thank you. By the way, is there a television in the room?

C: Yes, there is, we've got cable TV.

W: Oh, that's great.

C: Well, here's your room key. If you need anything else, more towels or anything, the office is open until midnight.

W: I wonder if I could get a wake-up call for 6:00 A.M. tomorrow?

C: Well, you'll find an alarm clock in your room. I am afraid that's the best we can do.

W: OK. Thanks again.

Review Unit 9

LISTEN TO THIS   PAGE 79

Enjoy the best of London's sights—from the top of an open-topped double-decker bus. Our full-day tour of London includes all the famous highlights and legendary landmarks of this historic city, such as the Tower of London, Big Ben, and Westminster Abbey. Relax and enjoy the fantastic views while listening to an entertaining and informative commentary from one of our expert guides. Recorded commentaries in languages other than English are available on request. Complimentary soft drinks are available.

Tickets are $35.00 for adults and $15.00 for children under 14. The tour lasts approximately two hours. Tickets can be purchased from the Information Center, selected hotels or, easiest of all, on the buses themselves. Keep your ticket and get on and off the tour bus to explore points of interest along the way. Or stop for lunch, which is not included in the tour, in one of London's many historic pubs. You can board any of our tour routes at over 90 different stops around the city. Buses run every 10 to 20 minutes.

The ticket price also includes a river cruise between Westminster Abbey and the Tower of London.

Hop on board for an unforgettable experience.

Unit 10

GIVE IT A TRY   **PAGE 81**

1. Asking who someone is

A: Who's that woman?
B: Which one?
A: The one in the purple sweater.
B: She's the one who just moved into my apartment building.

2. Identifying someone

A: Is Matt the one whose brother drives the red sports car?
B: Yes, that's right.

LISTEN TO THIS   **PAGE 82**

A: This is a great apartment.
G: I think so, too. Excuse me, but do I know you?
A: No. I'm Adam. I came with Carl. I don't really know anyone here. Carl's told me about most of his friends, but I can't match the names with the faces.
G: Well, let's see…OK, do you see that woman in the pink shirt?
A: Yeah.
G: That's Diana. She's the one who's moving to England next week. The party's for her.
A: OK. And who's that guy?
G: Which one?
A: The one in the green chair.
G: That's Cliff. He works in a bank.
A: Oh! Is he the man who owns the racehorses?
G: That's right. And do you see that guy with the beard?
A: Uh-huh.
G: That's Norm.
A: Is he the one who owns the restaurant?
G: No. Norm runs a dance studio. Let's see. Who else?
A: Wait. I don't want to embarrass myself. Which one is the hostess? Her name is Gina, right?
G: That's right. And I'm Gina. Nice to meet you. Glad you like my apartment!

GIVE IT A TRY   **PAGE 85**

1. Asking what someone is like

A: What do you think of Professor Vance?
B: He's boring.

2. Discussing qualities

A: My friend is great!
B: What makes her so great?
A: She's smart, so you can learn a lot from her.

LISTEN TO THIS   **PAGE 86**

B: I'm really mad at Mom and Dad.
G: Why? What did they do?
B: I asked them for a leather jacket for my birthday, and they just got me this stupid raincoat.
G: Oh, come on! It's a great coat.
B: I don't care! I wanted leather.

G: You know leather is expensive. Maybe they didn't have enough money.
B: I want to return it and get leather! All my friends have leather jackets.
G: They don't *all* have leather jackets.
B: Anyway, on your birthday, Mom and Dad gave you what you asked for.
G: That's true, but all I asked for was a new pair of jeans.
B: I hate this raincoat.
G: All right, how much is a leather jacket?
B: If I return this raincoat, all I need is another $50.00
G: OK, I'll lend you the $50.00, but you have to pay me back.
B: Great. Thank you so much, Sis!

Unit 11

GIVE IT A TRY   **PAGE 89**

1. Discussing experiences (1)

A: Have you ever tried snowboarding?
B: Yes, I have.
A: When?
B: I've done it lots of times.

2. Discussing experiences (2)

A: Have you ever tried mountain climbing?
B: Yes, I've done it lots of times.
A: When was the last time you went mountain climbing?
B: The last time was in the spring. I fell and hurt my leg.

3. Discussing experiences (3)

B: I tried snowboarding last winter.
A: Really? What was it like?
B: I was terrified at first.

LISTEN TO THIS   **PAGE 90**

1

You need to go somewhere where there's a fair bit of wind. Most people start with a two-liner. We spent hours running up and down the beach with it first, and then when we finally got to go out onto the water, I got the lines tangled up right away. Once you're up on your feet it's fine, but it took me about two hours the first time I tried it. It was very frustrating. I spent more time in the water than on the board! I was totally exhausted.

2

You need to go up somewhere really high. You never get tired of that wonderful feeling when you lift off and you're suspended in the air, thousands of feet above land with nothing but the sound of a gentle breeze. You feel so calm and peaceful. It's exhilarating. There's nothing like it!

3

You have to get up somewhere really high like a bridge or a tower. Or people sometimes use helicopters or hot air balloons. You have a body harness on. There's a bunch of cords attached to your middle. And then you jump!

If you're lucky you can get two or three really good bounces. Scary? You bet! It scared the life out of me! Terrific!

GIVE IT A TRY   **PAGE 93**

1. Telling a story

PRACTICE 1

A: Did I ever tell you about the time I found $150?
B: No. What happened?
A: I was taking the train to my judo class, when I saw a wallet on the seat next to me.

PRACTICE 2

A: I was taking the train to my judo class, when I saw a wallet on the seat next to me.
B: What did you do?
A: I gave it to a police officer when I got off.

2. Responding to someone's story

A: I turned the wallet into the police.
B: Good for you. That was really honest of you. Did they find the owner?

LISTEN TO THIS   **PAGE 94**

L: The most embarrassing thing that ever happened to me was a couple of years ago when I had just passed my driving test. I was driving through the city, very pleased and happy that I was driving on my own at last. There was quite a lot of traffic, but it wasn't too bad. In fact, the cars were moving very slowly which was fine for me. Then suddenly, the engine cut out.
P: The car stopped?
L: Yes! Well, I tried to start it up again, but I must have flooded the engine or something, because it just wouldn't start.
P: Oh, no! What did you do then?
L: I just didn't know what to do! I started to panic. I was in the middle of this really busy street, four lanes of traffic all around me, cars starting to line up behind me. I couldn't leave the car to go and get help. I just sat there, terrified.
P: That sounds awful. How embarrassing. And then what happened?
L: I suppose I was sitting there for at least ten minutes, but it seemed like an hour. And then a man came up out of the subway, saw what was happening, and came over to the car. And together we pushed the car over to the sidewalk, out of the way of the traffic. I was so relieved! I mean, he knew immediately what to do, and it was so simple, really.
P: Wow! What did you say to him?
L: Well, that was the funny thing. He couldn't speak any English, so I couldn't tell him how grateful I was. He just smiled and went away.
P: And you never saw him again?
L: No, I never saw him again.

Unit 12

GIVE IT A TRY   PAGE 97

1. Asking and giving opinions
A: What did you think of the movie?
B: I thought it was great.

2. Agreeing and disagreeing with opinions
A: What did you think of the movie?
B: I thought it was great.
A: So did I.

3. Giving reasons
A: What did you think of the movie?
B: I thought it was terrible.
A: What didn't you like about it?
B: It was too violent.

LISTEN TO THIS   PAGE 98

N: Welcome to another edition of *The Critical Eye*. Tonight, Jean Lovitt and Henry Pandit will give you their opinions on movies that will be opening soon in movie theaters across America.

H: Good evening, Jean.

J: Good evening, Henry. The first movie we're going to talk about tonight is *The Final Chapter*. Of course, I don't want to reveal too much, but it involves politics, murder, and a writer who uncovers some deadly secrets. This movie has everything—mystery, suspense, romance, and action. The problem is, the movie just doesn't work.

H: Why didn't you like it? I thought it was a great story. It kept my attention. There were a lot of details to remember, but it never got confusing. I thought the story was excellent.

J: You did? I didn't. I thought there were too many details. I found it really slow-moving and frustrating. I mean, they didn't need the romance between the detective and the writer.

H: That's true, but I think they wanted the characters to have more personality. I liked the characters more because of the romance.

J: Well, I didn't really like them because their relationship was just too slow-moving and boring. But, I thought the acting was good. Sam Foster's character was so real. I really liked his acting.

H: You did? I didn't. He was just OK. I really thought newcomer Cassie Lane, as the writer, was a bore! It's too bad—two good characters almost ruined by two bad acting jobs.

J: Well, I have to say, don't waste your money on this movie! The story is confusing and the characters are silly. Good acting couldn't save it!

H: And I say, the acting isn't that great, but the story and the characters are good enough to keep you entertained.

J: Now it's up to you. You've heard our opinions.

H: Now the final decision is yours.

GIVE IT A TRY   PAGE 101

1. Asking and giving opinions
A: What do you think about violence in movies?
B: Well, if you ask me, I think it is a problem.
A: I agree. Kids grow up thinking that it's OK to hurt people.
B: I think so, too.

2. Agreeing and adding a reason
A: Personally, I think romantic movies with happy endings are silly. They give people unrealistic expectations.
B: That's true. They're so superficial. They don't deal with real-life issues at all.

3. Seeing the other side
A: I think romantic movies with happy endings are silly. They give people unrealistic expectations.
B: That's true, but at least they don't encourage people to commit crimes and kill each other.

LISTEN TO THIS   PAGE 102

1

M: I see in the paper they're sending another rocket to Mars.
W: Oh, great. How much is that going to cost?
M: Oh, a couple of million, I guess.
W: Well, I think it's a big waste of money! There are poor countries and people starving on this planet. I think these space flights are stupid.
M: I don't think so. Because of them we have TV and weather satellites. Besides, we might have to live there some day.
W: Not me! I'm staying right here.

2

M: Your dog was barking all day yesterday. You shouldn't leave him at home like that.
W: That's only because my mother went out for the day. Usually he's a very quiet dog.
M: I don't agree with keeping pets. Especially when you live in apartments as small as ours. It's not good for animals to be in a small space like that. They need to run around in the fresh air.
W: Our dog is very happy at home with us. He has a very nice life! Only the best food, and lots of love and attention from me and my mom!
M: I suppose he keeps your mother company....
W: Yes, and it's good exercise for her when she takes him for a walk.
M: Well, I guess it's OK.... Just try not to leave him alone all day again, OK?

Review Unit 10

LISTEN TO THIS   PAGE 104

1

M: What a terrible waitress. No tip for her.
W: Well, I'm going to tip her. It's a tough job, especially at lunchtime. I used to be a waitress, so I know.

2

W: Our computer teacher is really boring. I'm sure I could teach better than that!
M: Oh yeah, since when are you an expert on computers?
W: I could teach a computer class if I wanted to!
M: You don't know what you're talking about! I'm glad I'm not in your class!

3

W: Hi! I'm Lisa! Are you a new student!
M: Yes...it's my first day...and I don't know anyone here.
W: Oh, I know everyone! And I've only been here two days. You'll soon make friends, don't worry. I'll introduce you to everyone I know!
M: That's really very kind of you. Thanks a lot.

Review Unit 11

LISTEN TO THIS   PAGE 104

This happened to me about four years ago in the summer. I was driving home from work one night. It was about eight in the evening. It was just getting dark. There was a beautiful sunset. I'd had a very difficult day at work, and I was looking forward to a nice relaxing evening at home.

I looked up at the sky, and I saw this string of bright lights. It looked like a group of airplanes. But I couldn't hear anything, and they were moving very slowly. Much more slowly than any airplanes I have ever seen. It was weird. Then suddenly, I saw more lights behind me, all different colors. So I stopped the car and got out. It was like a fireworks display—red, blue, green, and then these white lights in a circle around me. And it was very quiet. I stood there holding on to the car, waiting to see what would happen next. I wasn't scared. I just felt kind of fascinated. It must have gone on for perhaps an hour. Then suddenly, it all disappeared, and I was in the dark.

What did I do next? Well, I sat in my car for a while because the bright lights had made my eyes a bit funny. And I tried to calm down. In my mind, I was trying to find a rational explanation for it. But to tell you the truth, to this day, I have no idea what it was.

Review Unit 12

M: The question of censorship on the Internet always raises a lot of controversy. Tonight we'll hear opinions from people from four different countries. Our guests tonight are Roger from Canada, Tomomi from Japan, Antonio from Italy, and Frank from Hong Kong. Roger, let's start with you.

R: I'm against any sort of government censorship on the Internet. I think the Internet should be freely available to everyone who wants to express his or opinion. Once you start trying to control it, it just becomes a political tool for the government.

T: I disagree with Roger. I think that there are a lot of harmful sites on the Web that are not suitable for children. I think it's fine if parents or schools want to control what children can access on the Internet.

M: That's a good point. So you think censorship is OK. Antonio, what do you think?

A: I think Tomomi is right. We do need some kind of censorship to make sure that the Internet is educational and not used for criminal purposes.

M: Frank, what's your opinion?

F: Well, I know it sounds strange, but I think that children have to learn to distinguish good and bad on the Internet, just as they do in real life. We can't protect them all the time. They have to learn to protect themselves. So I guess I am against any kind of censorship.

M: Thank you, guests. You've heard some opinions from around the world. Now we want to hear your opinions. E-mail us with your comments at www.news.com.